THE LAST BEST HOPE

The Greatest Speeches of Ronald Reagan

THE LAST BEST HOPE

The Greatest Speeches of Ronald Reagan

Humanix Books

www.humanixbooks.com

Humanix Books

The Last Best Hope
Copyright © 2016 by Humanix Books
All rights reserved

Introduction by Michael Reagan previously published in
The Greatest Speeches of Ronald Reagan © 2002 Newsmax

Humanix Books, P.O. Box 20989, West Palm Beach, FL 33416, USA
www.humanixbooks.com | info@humanixbooks.com

Library of Congress Cataloging-in-Publication Data

Names: Reagan, Ronald.
Title: The last best hope : the greatest speeches of Ronald Reagan /
    introduction by Michael Reagan.
Description: West Palm Beach, FL : Humanix Books, 2016.
Identifiers: LCCN 2015041364 (print) | LCCN 2015041775 (ebook) | ISBN
    9781630060497 (hardcover) | ISBN 9781630060503 (ebook) | ISBN
    9781630060503 ()
Subjects: LCSH: Reagan, Ronald--Oratory. | United States--Politics and
    government--1981-1989. | United States--Foreign relations--1981-1989. |
    Speeches, addresses, etc., American.
Classification: LCC E838.5 .R435 2016 (print) | LCC E838.5 (ebook) | DDC
    973.927092--dc23
LC record available at http://lccn.loc.gov/2015041364

Cover photo: Corbis-42-23040047
Interior design: Ben Davis

Humanix Books is a division of Humanix Publishing, LLC. Its trademark, consisting of the words "Humanix" is registered in the Patent and Trademark Office and in other countries

ISBN: 978-1-63006-049-7 (Paperback)
ISBN: 978-1-63006-050-3 (E-book)

Printed in the United States of America

Contents

Introduction

If you want to understand what Ronald Reagan really accom-plished, you need to get on a plane and go to those Eastern Bloc countries that were under communist control for so many, many years.

Over a decade after the fall of the Berlin Wall, you'll still find a blighted land of gray people and gray buildings. It's as if a great plague had sapped the vitality and spirit of a continent, and only now are the land and its people beginning to recover.

When Ronald Reagan became president in 1981, totalitarian communism was at its zenith. From Europe, to Africa, to Asia, to South America, country after country had fallen under the evil spell of Marx and Lenin and Stalin and Khrushchev—and whatever the communists couldn't control, they threatened to destroy with thousands of hydrogen bombs.

At the same time, America seemed to be in decline, with 8 million people out of work, inflation over 12 percent, and a prime interest rate of over 20 percent. America seemed to be losing its way.

And then came Ronald Reagan.

He spoke of renewal and hope; of defeating communism, not accommodating it; of economically revitalizing America with lower taxes and less government; and of the spiritual commitment and faith. When it was unfashionable and corny, he spoke of the values that had made America great and noble and wealthy, and of how we must return to those values. He infused millions—both in the United States and around the world—with new hope and a new spirit.

That alone would have been accomplishment enough, but even more amazingly, Ronald Reagan did precisely what he said he would: he revitalized America, decreased the burden of bloated government, and defeated communism.

In March of 1983—when the power of the Soviet Union seemed unassailable and communism held dominion over nearly 2 billion human souls—Ronald Reagan declared in his famous "Evil Empire" speech in Florida:

"I believe that communism is another sad, bizarre chapter in human history whose last pages even now are being written."

It was an incredibly bold statement to make in the context of the times. The Soviet Union had been in existence for over 65 years and showed no signs of retreating, much less collapsing. Most people dismissed Ronald Reagan's statement as mere rhetoric or simply a clever turn of phrase. Oh, perhaps one day the Soviet Empire would collapse, like other empires before it, but certainly not in the lifetime of anyone then living.

Six and a half years later, the Berlin Wall was torn down and totalitarian communism was collapsing everywhere throughout the world. The Soviet Empire was dead, not in centuries or even decades, but in a mere handful of years. The simple words that Ronald Reagan had spoken in 1983 had become the truth.

Acting with enormous foresight and courage, Ronald Reagan had rebuilt America's battered military into the greatest power the world had ever known, and sickly communist economies simply couldn't keep pace.

By the time Ronald Reagan left office in 1989, his other promises had been kept as well. Taxes had been slashed, government had shrunk, and inflation and unemployment were at record lows.

Before Reagan, communists were challenging America everywhere in the world. After Reagan, America was unchallengeable.

Before Reagan, it was unfashionable to be a conservative. After him, it was hip.

Before Reagan, it was unfashionable to openly proclaim your love for your country, particularly on college campuses. After Reagan, patriotism was again respectable.

Before Reagan, people were ashamed to admit that they had strong religious beliefs. After Reagan, millions of Americans again proudly proclaimed their faith, and there was a great re-awakening of religious fervor on colleges throughout our country.

All of these were Reagan's gifts to America. But most of all, he helped this country to believe in itself again. As always, the Great Communicator said it best himself:

"America has bred kindliness into our people unmatched any-where. We are not a sick society. A sick society could not produce the men that set foot on the moon, or who are now circling the earth above us in Skylab. A sick society bereft of morality and courage did not produce the men who went through those years of torture and captivity in Vietnam. Where did we find such men? They are typical of this land. We found them in our streets, in the offices, the shops and the working places of our country and on the farms." (Ronald Reagan, "We Will Be a City Upon a Hill," speech to the First Conservative Political Action Conference, January 1974)

The book you are holding in your hands spans 30 years of Ronald Reagan's life and one of the most tumultuous periods in American history. In the 28 speeches in this volume, you'll discover gem after gem, each filled with wit and insight. I hope you'll enjoy it as much as I did, and gain a deeper insight into the character and spirit of one of the greatest Americans in our history.

Michael Reagan
Los Angeles, California

"What we can borrow from Ronald Reagan is that great sense of optimism. He led by building on the strengths of America, not running America down."

Rudy Giuliani, from The Republicans' First
Presidential Candidates Debate, 2007

1

A TIME FOR CHOOSING

Into the early 1960s, Ronald Reagan was widely known as an actor, but that changed in 1964 when Reagan would make a seamless segue from the silver screen into a much different role–that of "the Great Communicator."

Departing from his liberal tenets, Reagan entered the political arena in a philosophical comfort-zone in the Republican Party. Reagan was later credited with launching the modern conservative movement. Reagan agreed to help Barry Goldwater in the final push of his presidential campaign against Lyndon B. Johnson.

Airing on October 27, 1964, "A Time for Choosing" was a pre-recorded speech that highlighted Reagan's unique gift for rhetoric. In what became known as "the Speech," Reagan attacked liberalism, but showed his partisan approach.

Though Goldwater lost the election, this speech would be remembered as one of the most emotionally charged, galvanizing speeches in our nation's history–one that immediately catapulted Ronald Reagan to the forefront of politics, and placed among America's most beloved presidents to date.

Nationwide Televised Address for
Barry Goldwater Presidential Campaign

October 27, 1964

I am going to talk of controversial things. I make no apology for this.

It's time we asked ourselves if we still know the freedoms intended for us by the Founding Fathers. James Madison said, "We base all our experiments on the capacity of mankind for self-government."

This idea that government was beholden to the people, that it had no other source of power, is still the newest, most unique idea in all the long history of man's relation to man. This is the issue of this election: whether we believe in our capacity for self-government or whether we abandon the American Revolution and confess that a little intellectual elite in a far-distant capital can plan our lives for us better than we can plan them ourselves.

You and I are told we must choose between a left and right, but I suggest there is no such thing as a left or right. There is only an up or down. Up to man's age-old dream, the maximum of individual freedom consistent with order, or down to the ant heap of totalitarianism. Regardless of their sincerity, their humanitarian motives, those who would sacrifice freedom for security have embarked on this downward path. Plutarch warned, "The real destroyer of the liberties of the people is he who spreads among them bounties, donations and benefits."

The Founding Fathers knew a government can't control the economy without controlling people. And they knew when a government sets out to do that, it must use force and coercion to achieve its purpose. So we have come to a time for choosing.

Public servants say, always with the best of intentions, "What greater service we could render if only we had a little more money and a little more power." But the truth is that outside of its legitimate function, government does nothing as well or as economically as the private sector.

Yet anytime you and I question the schemes of the do-gooders, we're denounced as being opposed to their humanitarian goals. It seems impossible to legitimately debate their solutions with the assumption that all of us share the desire to help the less fortunate. They tell us we're always "against," never "for" anything.

We are for a provision that destitution should not follow unemployment by reason of old age, and to that end we have accepted Social Security as a step toward meeting the problem. However, we are against those entrusted with this program when they practice deception regarding its fiscal shortcomings, when they charge that any criticism of the program means that we want to end payments.

We are for aiding our allies by sharing our material blessings with nations which share our fundamental beliefs, but we are against doling out money government to government, creating bureaucracy, if not socialism, all over the world.

We need true tax reform that will at least make a start toward restoring for our children the American Dream that wealth is denied to no one, that each individual has the right to fly as high as his strength and ability will take him, but we cannot have such reform while our tax policy is engineered by people who view the tax as a means of achieving changes in our social structure.

Have we the courage and the will to face up to the immorality and discrimination of the progressive tax and demand a return to traditional proportionate taxation? Today in our country, the tax collector's share is thirty-seven cents of every dollar earned. Freedom has never been so fragile, so close to slipping from our grasp.

Are you willing to spend time studying the issues, making yourself aware, and then conveying that information to family and friends? Will you resist the temptation to get a government handout for your community? Realize that the doctor's fight against socialized medicine is your fight. We can't socialize the doctors without socializing the patients. Recognize that government invasion of public power is eventually an assault upon your own business. If some among you fear taking a stand because you are afraid of reprisals from customers, clients, or even government, recognize that you are just feeding the crocodile, hoping he'll eat you last.

If all of this seems like a great deal of trouble, think what's at stake. We are faced with the most evil enemy mankind has known in his long climb from the swamp to the stars. There can be no security anywhere in the Free World if there is no fiscal and economic stability within the United States. Those who ask us to trade our freedom for the soup kitchen of the welfare state are architects of a policy of accommodation.

They say the world has become too complex for simple answers. They are wrong. There are no easy answers, but there are simple answers. We must have the courage to do what we know is morally right. Winston Churchill said that "the destiny of man is not measured by material computation. When great forces are on the move in the world, we learn we are spirits—not animals." And he said, "There is something going on in time and space, and beyond time and space, which, whether we like it or not, spells duty."

You and I have a rendezvous with destiny. We will preserve for our children this, the last best hope of man on earth, or we will sentence them to take the first step into a thousand years of darkness. If we fail, at least let our children and our children's children say of us we justified our brief moment here. We did all that could be done.

2

THE PROBLEM OF GOVERNMENT

Still riding the wave of popularity inspired by his 1964 "A Time for Choosing" speech, Ronald Reagan was nominated as the Republican party's candidate for governor of California. After touring the state for six months, he announced his gubernatorial bid on television.

Reagan focused on two issues–welfare and Berkeley. He resented the so-called welfare "bums," and was even angrier toward the powers at Berkeley for allowing "spoiled" students to disrupt campus activities in protest of the Vietnam War.

While the incumbent, Edmund "Pat" Brown, dismissed him as an actor with no political experience, Reagan called himself a "citizen politician." His criticism of Brown's soft approach to the "mess at Berkeley" and lawlessness in general, as well as his support for government programs, won him the lion's share of votes.

At one minute after midnight on January 2, 1967, Ronald Reagan was sworn in as governor of California.

First Address as Governor of California

JANUARY 5, 1967

———

To a number of us, this is a first and hence a solemn and momentous occasion, and yet, on the broad page of state and national history, what is taking place here is almost commonplace routine. We are participating in the orderly transfer of administrative authority by direction of the people. And this is the simple magic which makes a commonplace routine a near miracle to many of the world's inhabitants: the continuing fact that the people, by democratic process, can delegate this power yet retain custody of it.

Perhaps you and I have lived with this miracle too long to be properly appreciative. Freedom is a fragile thing and is never more than one generation away from extinction. It is not ours by inheritance; it must be fought for and defended constantly by each generation, for it comes only once to a people. Those who have known freedom and then lost it have never known it again. Knowing this, it is hard to explain those who even today would question the people's capacity for self-rule. Will they answer this: If no one among us is capable of governing himself, then who among us has the capacity to govern someone else? Using the temporary authority granted by the people, an increasing number lately have sought to control the means of production, as if this could be done without eventually controlling those who produce. Always this is explained as necessary to the people's welfare. But "The deterioration of every government begins with the decay of the principle upon which it was founded." This is as true today as it was when it was written in 1748 [by Montesquieu].

Government is the people's business, and every man, woman, and child becomes a shareholder with the first penny of tax paid.

With all the profound wording of the Constitution, probably the most meaningful words are the first three: "We the People." Those of us here today who have been elected to constitutional office or legislative position are in that three-word phrase. We are of the people, chosen by them to see that no permanent structure of government ever encroaches on freedom or assumes a power beyond that freely granted by the people. We stand between the taxpayer and the tax spender.

It is inconceivable to me that anyone could accept this delegated authority without asking God's help. I pray that we who legislate and administer will be granted wisdom and strength beyond our own limited power; that with Divine guidance we can avoid easy expedients as we work to build a state where liberty under law and justice can triumph, where compassion can govern, and wherein the people can participate and prosper because of their government and not in spite of it.

The path we will chart is not an easy one. It demands much of those chosen to govern, but also from those who did the choosing. And let there be no mistake about this: We have come to a crossroad, a time of decision, and the path we follow turns away from any idea that government and those who serve it are omnipotent. It is a path impossible to follow unless we have faith in the collective wisdom and genius of the people. Along this path government will lead but not rule, listen but not lecture. It is the path of a creative society.

A number of problems were discussed during the campaign, and I see no reason to change the subject now. Campaign oratory on the issues of crime, pollution of air and water, conservation, welfare, and expanded educational facilities does not mean the issues will go away because the campaign has ended. Problems remain to be solved and they challenge all of us. Government will lead, of course, but the answer must come from all of you.

We will make specific proposals and we will solicit other ideas. In the area of crime, where we have double our proportionate share, we will propose legislation to give back to local communities the right to pass and enforce ordinances which will enable the police to more adequately protect these communities. Legislation already drafted will be submitted, calling upon the Legislature clearly to state in the future whether newly adopted laws are intended to preempt the right of local governments to legislate in the same field. Hopefully, this will free judges from having to guess the intent of those who passed the legislation in the first place.

At the same time, I pledge my support and fullest effort to a plan which will remove from politics, once and for all, the appointment of judges—not that I believe I'll be overburdened with making judicial appointments in the immediate future.

Just as we assume a responsibility to guard our young people up to a certain age from the possible harmful effects of alcohol and tobacco, so do I believe we have a right and a responsibility to protect them from the even more harmful effects of exposure to smut and pornography. We can and must frame legislation that will accomplish this purpose without endangering freedom of speech and the press.

When fiscally feasible, we hope to create a California crime technological foundation utilizing both public and private resources in a major effort to employ the most scientific techniques to control crime. At such a time, we should explore the idea of a state police academy to assure that police from even the smallest communities can have the most advanced training. We lead the nation in many things; we are going to stop leading in crime. Californians should be able to walk our streets safely day or night. The law abiding are entitled to at least as much protection as the lawbreakers.

While on the subject of crime, those with a grievance can seek redress in the courts or legislature, but not in the streets. Lawlessness by the mob, as with the individual, will not be tolerated. We will act firmly and quickly to put down riot or insurrection wherever and whenever the situation requires.

Welfare is another of our major problems. We are a humane and generous people and we accept without reservation our obligation to help the aged, disabled and those unfortunates who, through no fault of their own, must depend on their fellow man. But we are not going to perpetuate poverty by substituting a permanent dole for a paycheck. There is no humanity or charity in destroying self-reliance, dignity and self-respect—the very substance of moral fiber.

We seek reforms that will, wherever possible, change relief check to paycheck. Spencer Williams, administrator of Health and Welfare, is assessing the amount of work that could be done in public installations by welfare recipients. This is not being done in any punitive sense, but as a beginning step in rehabilitation to give the individual the self-respect that goes with performing a useful service.

But this is not the ultimate answer. Only private industry in the last analysis can provide jobs with a future. Lieutenant Governor Robert Finch will be liaison between government and the private sector in an all-out program of job training and education leading to real employment.

A truly great citizen of our state and a fine American, Mr. H. C. McClellan, has agreed to institute a statewide program patterned after the one he directed so successfully in the "curfew area" of Los Angeles. There, in the year and a half since the tragic riots, fully half of the unemployed have been channeled into productive jobs in private industry, and more than 2,600 businesses are involved. Mr. McClellan will be serving without pay, and the entire statewide program will be privately financed. While it will be directed at all who lack opportunity, it offers hope especially to those minorities who have a disproportionate share of poverty and unemployment.

In the whole area of welfare, everything will be done to reduce administrative overhead, cut red tape, and return control as much as possible to the county level. And the goal will be investment in, and salvage of, human beings.

This administration will cooperate with the State Superintendent of Public Instruction in his expressed desires to return more control of curriculum and selection of textbooks to local school districts. We will support his efforts to make recruitment of out-of-state teachers less difficult.

In the subject of education, hundreds of thousands of young men and women will receive an education in our state colleges and universities. We are proud of our ability to provide this opportunity for our youth, and we believe it is no denial of academic freedom to provide this education within a framework of reasonable rules and regulations. Nor is it a violation of individual rights to require obedience to these rules and regulations or to insist that those unwilling to abide by them should get their education elsewhere.

It does not constitute political interference with intellectual freedom for the taxpaying citizens who support the college and university systems to ask that, in addition to teaching, they build character on accepted moral and ethical standards.

Just as a man is entitled to a voice in government, so he should certainly have that right in the very personal matter of earning a living. I have always supported the principle of the union shop, even though that includes a certain amount of compulsion with regard to union membership. For that reason it seems to me that government must accept a responsibility for safeguarding each union member's democratic rights within his union. For that reason we will submit legislative proposals to guarantee each union member a secret ballot in his union on policy matters and the use of union dues.

There is also need for a mediation service in labor management disputes not covered by existing law. There are improvements to be made in workmen's compensation, in death benefits and benefits to the permanently disabled. At the same time, a tightening of procedures is needed to free business from some unjust burdens.

A close liaison with our congressional representatives in Washington, both Democratic and Republican, is needed so that we can help bring about beneficial changes in Social Security, secure less restrictive controls on federal grants, and work for a tax retention plan that will keep some of our federal taxes here for our use, with no strings attached. We should strive also to get tax credits for our people to help defray the cost of sending their children to college.

We will support a bipartisan effort to lift the archaic 160-acre limitation imposed by the federal government on irrigated farms. Restrictive labor policies should never again be the cause of crops rotting in the fields for lack of harvesters.

Here in our own Capitol, we will seek solutions to the problems of unrealistic taxes which threaten economic ruin to our biggest industry. We will work with the farmer as we will with business, industry and labor to provide a better business climate so that they may prosper and we all may prosper.

There are other problems and possible problems facing us. One such is now pending before the United States Supreme Court. I believe it would be inappropriate to discuss that matter now. We will, however, be prepared with remedial legislation we devoutly hope will be satisfactory to all of our citizens if court rulings make this necessary.

This is only a partial accounting of our problems and our dreams for the future. California, with its climate, its resources and its wealth of young, aggressive, talented people, must never take second place. We can provide jobs for all our people who will work, and we can have honest government at a price we can afford. Indeed, unless we accomplish this, our problems will go unsolved, our dreams unfulfilled, and we will know the taste of ashes.

I have put off until last what is by no means least among our problems. Our fiscal situation has a sorry similarity to the situation of a jetliner out over the North Atlantic, Paris-bound.

The pilot announced he had news, some good, some bad, and he would give the bad news first. They had lost radio contact; their compass and altimeter were not working; they didn't know their altitude, direction, or where they were headed. Then he gave the good news: They had a hundred-mile-an-hour tail wind and they were ahead of schedule.

Our fiscal year began July 1 and will end on the coming June 30, six months from now. The present budget for this twelve-month period is $4.6 billion, an all-time high for any of the fifty states. When this budget was presented, it was admittedly in excess of the estimated tax revenues for the year. It was adopted with the assurance that a change in bookkeeping procedures would solve this imbalance.

With half the year gone, and faced now with the job of planning next year's budget, we have an estimate provided by the experienced personnel of the Department of Finance. We have also an explanation of how a change in bookkeeping could seemingly balance a budget that called for spending $400 million more than we would take in.

Very simply, it was just another one-time windfall, a gimmick that solved nothing but only postponed the day of reckoning. We are financing the twelve-month spending with fifteen-month income. All the tax revenues for the first quarter of next year—July, August, and September—will be used to finance this year's expenses up to June 30. And incidentally, even that isn't enough, because we will still have a deficit of some $63 million.

Now, with the budget established at its present level, we are told that it, of course, must be increased next year to meet the added problems of population growth and inflation. But the magic of the changed bookkeeping is all used up. We are back to only twelve months' income for twelve months' spending. Almost automatically we are being advised of all the new and increased taxes which, if adopted, will solve the problem. Curiously enough, another one-time windfall is being urged. If we switch to with-holding of personal income tax, we will collect two years' taxes the first year and postpone our moment of truth perhaps until everyone forgets we did not cause the problem, we only inherited it. Or maybe we are to stall, hoping a rich uncle will remember us in his will.

If we accept the present budget as absolutely necessary and add on projected increases plus funding for property tax relief (which I believe is absolutely essential and for which we are preparing a detailed and comprehensive program), our deficit in the coming year would reach three-quarters of a billion dollars.

But Californians are already burdened with combined state and local taxes $113 per capita higher than the national average. Our property tax contributes to a slump in the real estate and building trades industries and makes it well-nigh impossible for many citizens to continue owning their own homes.

For many years now, you and I have been shushed like children and told there are no simple answers to the complex problems which are beyond our comprehension.

Well, the truth is there are simple answers. They just are not easy ones. The time has come for us to decide whether collectively we can afford everything and anything we think of simply because we think of it. The time has come to run a check to see if all the services government provides were in answer to demands or were just goodies dreamed up for our supposed betterment. The time has come to match outgo to income, instead of always doing it the other way around.

The cost of California's government is too high; it adversely affects our business climate. We have a phenomenal growth with hundreds of thousands of people joining us each year. Of course, the overall cost of government must go up to provide necessary services for these newcomers, but growth should mean increased prosperity and thus a lightening of the load each individual must bear. If this isn't true, then you and I should be planning how we can put up a fence along the Colorado River and seal our borders.

Well, we aren't going to do that. We are going to squeeze and cut and trim until we reduce the cost of government. It won't be easy, nor will it be pleasant, and it will involve every department of government, starting with the governor's office. I have already informed the Legislature of the reorganization we hope to effect with their help in the executive branch and I have asked for their cooperation and support.

The new director of Finance is in complete agreement that we turn to additional sources of revenue only if it becomes clear that economies alone cannot balance the budget.

Disraeli said: "Man is not a creature of circumstances. Circumstances are the creatures of men." You and I will shape our circumstances to fit our needs.

Let me reaffirm a promise made during the months of campaigning. I believe in your right to know all the facts concerning the people's business. Independent firms are making an audit of state finances. When it is completed, you will have that audit. You will have all the information you need to make the decisions which must be made. This is not just a problem for the administration, it is a problem for all of us to solve together. I know that you can face any prospect and do anything that has to be done as long as you know the truth of what you are up against.

We will put our fiscal house in order. And as we do, we will build those things we need to make our state a better place in which to live and we will enjoy them more, knowing we can afford them and they are paid for.

If, in glancing aloft, some of you were puzzled by the small size of our state flag, there is an explanation. That flag was carried into battle in Vietnam by young men of California. Many will not be coming home. One did: Sergeant Robert Howell, grievously wounded. He brought that flag back. I thought we would be proud to have it fly over the Capitol today. It might even serve to put our problems in better perspective. It might remind us of the need to give our sons and daughters a cause to believe in and banners to follow.

If this is a dream, it is a good dream, worthy of our generation and worth passing on to the next.

Let this day mark the beginning.

3

WE WILL BE A CITY
UPON A HILL

Toward the close of his second term as governor of California, Ronald Reagan was invited to speak at the first Conservative Political Action Conference (CPAC), hosted by the American Conservative Union (ACU)–the oldest conservative advocate and lobbying organization in the United States.

When Reagan stepped up to the podium, conservatism seemed outdated in the face of the sixty's love generation. A loss for Goldwater was a loss for the conservative movement, and the group needed someone to spread its message in a new way. In Reagan, they found that and more.

Reagan's message came through loud and clear: from our Founding Fathers signing that sacred document, to those fighting for racial equality, the freedom and independence in the U.S. still serves as a model for all nations.

There, in front of his esteemed constituents, he cemented his role as the new conservative hope, and his candidacy in future elections.

First Conservative Political Action Conference

JANUARY 25, 1974

—————

There are three men here tonight I am very proud to introduce. It was a year ago this coming February when this country had its spirits lifted as they have never been lifted in many years. This happened when planes began landing on American soil and in the Philippines, bringing back men who had lived with honor for many miserable years in North Vietnam prisons. Three of those men are here tonight: John McCain, Bill Lawrence, and Ed Martin. It is an honor to be here tonight. I am proud that you asked me, and I feel more than a little humble in the presence of this distinguished company.

There are men here tonight who, through their wisdom, their foresight and their courage, have earned the right to be regarded as prophets of our philosophy. Indeed, they are prophets of our times. In years past, when others were silent or too blind to the facts, they spoke up forcefully and fearlessly for what they believed to be right. A decade has passed since Barry Goldwater walked a lonely path across this land reminding us that even a land as rich as ours can't go on forever borrowing against the future, leaving a legacy of debt for another generation and causing a runaway inflation to erode the savings and reduce the standard of living. Voices have been raised trying to rekindle in our country all of the great ideas and principles which set this nation apart from all the others that preceded it, but louder and more strident voices utter easily sold clichés.

Cartoonists with acid-tipped pens portray some of the reminders of our heritage and our destiny as old-fashioned. They say that we are trying to retreat into a past that actually never existed. Looking to the past in an effort to keep our country from repeating the errors of history is termed by them as "taking the country back to McKinley." Of course, I never found that was so bad—under McKinley we freed Cuba. On the span of history, we are still thought of as a young, upstart country, celebrating soon only our second century as a nation, and yet we are the oldest continuing republic in the world.

I thought that tonight, rather than talking on the subjects you are discussing, or trying to find something new to say, it might be appropriate to reflect a bit on our heritage.

You can call it mysticism if you want to, but I have always believed that there was some Divine plan that placed this great continent between two oceans, to be sought out by those who were possessed of an abiding love of freedom and a special kind of courage.

This was true of those who pioneered the great wilderness in the beginning of this country, as it is also true of those later immigrants who were willing to leave the land of their birth and come to a land where even the language was unknown to them. Call it chauvinistic, but our heritage does set us apart. Some years ago a writer, who happened to be an avid student of history, told me a story about that day in the little hall in Philadelphia where honorable men, hard-pressed by a king who was flouting the very law they were willing to obey, debated whether they should take the fateful step of declaring their independence from that king. I was told by this man that the story could be found in the writings of Jefferson. I confess I never researched or made an effort to verify it. Perhaps it is only legend. But story or legend, he described the atmosphere, the strain, the debate, and that as men for the first time faced the consequences of such an irretrievable act, the walls resounded with the dread word of treason and its price—the gallows and the headman's axe.

As the day wore on, the issue hung in the balance, and then, according to the story, a man rose in the small gallery. He was not a young man and was obviously calling on all the energy he could muster. Citing the grievances that had brought them to this moment, he said, "Sign that parchment. They may turn every tree into a gallows, every home into a grave, and yet the words of that parchment can never die. For the mechanic in his workshop, they will be words of hope; to the slave in the mines, freedom." And he added, "If my hands were freezing in death, I would sign that parchment with my last ounce of strength. Sign, sign if the next moment the noose is around your neck, sign even if the hall is ringing with the sound of headman's axe, for that parchment will be the textbook of freedom, the bible of the rights of man forever." And then, it is said, he fell back, exhausted. But fifty-six delegates, swept by his eloquence, signed the Declaration of Independence, a document destined to be as immortal as any work of man can be. And according to the story, when they turned to thank him for his timely oratory, he could not be found, nor were there any who knew who he was or how he had come in or gone out through the locked and guarded doors.

Well, as I say, whether story or legend, the signing of the document that day in Independence Hall was miracle enough. Fifty-six men, a little band—so unique we have never seen their like since—pledged their lives, their fortunes and their sacred honor. Sixteen gave their lives, most gave their fortunes, and all of them preserved their sacred honor. What manner of men were they? Certainly they were not an unwashed, revolutionary rebel, nor were they adventurers in a heroic mood. Twenty-four were lawyers and jurists, eleven were merchants and tradesmen, nine were farmers. They were men who would achieve security but valued freedom more.

And what price did they pay? John Hart was driven from the side of his desperately ill wife. After more than a year of living almost as an animal in the forest and in caves, he returned to find his wife had died and his children had vanished. He never saw them again, his property was destroyed, and he died of a broken heart—but with no regret, only pride in the part he had played that day in Independence Hall. Carter Braxton of Virginia lost all his ships—they were sold to pay his debts. He died in rags. So it was with Ellery, Clymer, Hall, Walton, Gwinnett, Rut-ledge, Morris, Livingston, and Middleton. Nelson, learning that Cornwallis was using his home for a headquarters, personally begged Washington to fire on him and destroy his home—he died bankrupt. It has never been reported that any of these men ever expressed bitterness or renounced their action as not worth the price. Fifty-six rank-and-file, ordinary citizens had founded a nation that grew from sea to shining sea, 5 million farms, quiet villages, cities that never sleep—all done without an area redevelopment plan, urban renewal, or a rural legal assistance program.

Now we are a nation of 211 million people, with a pedigree that includes bloodlines from every corner of the world. We have shed that American-melting-pot blood in every corner of the world, usually in defense of someone's freedom. Those who remained of that remarkable band we call our Founding Fathers tied up some of the loose ends about a dozen years after the Revolution. It had been the first revolution in all man's history that did not just exchange one set of rulers for another. This had been a philosophical revolution. The culmination of men's dreams for six thousand years were formalized with the Constitution, probably the most unique document ever drawn in the long history of man's relation to man.

I know there have been other constitutions; new ones are being drawn today by newly emerging nations. Most of them, even the one of the Soviet Union, contains many of the same guarantees as our own Constitution, and still there is a difference. The difference is so subtle that we often overlook it, but it is so great that it tells the whole story. Those other constitutions say "Government grants you these rights" and ours says "You are born with these rights, they are yours by the grace of God, and no government on earth can take them from you."

Lord Acton of England, who once said, "Power corrupts, and absolute power corrupts absolutely," would say of that document, "They had solved with astonishing ease and unduplicated success two problems which had heretofore baffled the capacity of the most enlightened nations. They had contrived a system of federal government which prodigiously increased national power and yet respected local liberties and authorities, and they had founded it on a principle of equality without surrendering the securities of property or freedom." Never in any society has the preeminence of the individual been so firmly established and given such a priority.

In less than twenty years we would go to war because the God-given rights of the American sailors, as defined in the Constitution, were being violated by a foreign power. We served notice then on the world that all of us together would act collectively to safeguard the rights of even the least among us. But still, in an older, cynical world, they were not convinced. The great powers of Europe still had the idea that one day this great continent would be open again to colonizing, and they would come over and divide us up.

In the meantime, men who yearned to breathe free were making their way to our shores. Among them was a young refugee from the Austro-Hungarian Empire. He had been a leader in an attempt to free Hungary from Austrian rule. The attempt had failed and he fled to escape execution. In America, this young Hungarian, Koscha by name, became an importer by trade and took out his first citizenship papers. One day, business took him to a Mediterranean port. There was a large Austrian warship under the command of an admiral in the harbor. He had a manservant with him. He had described to this manservant what the flag of his new country looked like. Word was passed to the Austrian warship that this revolutionary was there, and in the night he was kidnapped and taken aboard that large ship. This man's servant, desperate, walking up and down the harbor, suddenly spied a flag that resembled the description he had heard. It was a small

American war sloop. He went aboard and told Captain Ingraham, of that war sloop, his story. Captain Ingraham went to the American Consul. When the American Consul learned that Koscha had only taken out his first citizenship papers, the consul washed his hands of the incident. Captain Ingraham said, "I am the senior officer in this port and I believe, under my oath of my office, that I owe this man the protection of our flag."

He went aboard the Austrian warship and demanded to see their prisoner, our citizen. The admiral was amused, but they brought the man on deck. He was in chains and had been badly beaten. Captain Ingraham said, "I can hear him better without those chains," and the chains were removed. He walked over and said to Koscha, "I will ask you one question; consider your answer carefully. Do you ask the protection of the American flag?" Koscha nodded dumbly, "Yes," and the Captain said, "You shall have it." He went back and told the frightened consul what he had done. Later in the day three more Austrian ships sailed into harbor. It looked as though the four were getting ready to leave. Captain Ingraham sent a junior officer over to the Austrian flagship to tell the admiral that any attempt to leave that harbor with our citizen aboard would be resisted with appropriate force. He said that he would expect a satisfactory answer by four o'clock that afternoon. As the hour neared, they looked at each other through the glasses. As it struck four, he had them roll the cannons into the ports and had then light the tapers with which they would set off the cannons—one little sloop. Suddenly the lookout tower called out and said, "They are lowering a boat," and they rowed Koscha over to the little American ship.

Captain Ingraham then went below and wrote his letter of resignation to the United States Navy. In it he said, "I did what I thought my oath of office required, but if I have embarrassed my country in any way, I resign." His resignation was refused in the United States Senate with these words: "This battle that was never fought may turn out to be the most important battle in our

Nation's history." Incidentally, there is to this day, and I hope there always will be, a USS Ingraham in the United States Navy.

I did not tell that story out of any desire to be narrowly chauvinistic or to glorify aggressive militarism, but it is an example of government meeting its highest responsibility.

In recent years we have been treated to a rash of noble-sounding phrases. Some of them sound good, but they don't hold up under close analysis. Take, for instance, the slogan so frequently uttered by the young senator from Massachusetts, "The greatest good for the greatest number." Certainly under that slogan, no modern-day Captain Ingraham would risk even the smallest craft and crew for a single citizen. Every dictator who ever lived has justified the enslavement of his people on the theory of what was good for the majority.

We are not a warlike people. Nor is our history filled with tales of aggressive adventures and imperialism, which might come as a shock to some of the placard painters in our modern demonstrations. The lesson of Vietnam, I think, should be that never again will young Americans be asked to fight and possibly die for a cause unless that cause is so meaningful that we, as a nation, pledge our full resources to achieve victory as quickly as possible.

I realize that such a pronouncement, of course, would possibly be laying one open to the charge of warmongering—but that would also be ridiculous. My generation has paid a higher price and has fought harder for freedom than any generation that has ever lived. We have known four wars in a single lifetime. All were horrible. All could have been avoided if, at a particular moment in time, we had made it plain that we subscribed to the words of John Stuart Mill when he said that "war is an ugly thing, but not the ugliest of things."

The decayed and degraded state of moral and patriotic feeling which thinks nothing is worth a war is worse. The man who has nothing which he cares about more than his personal safety is a miserable creature and has no chance of being free unless made and kept so by the exertions of better men than himself.

The widespread disaffection with things military is only a part of the philosophical division in our land today. I must say to you who have recently or presently are still receiving an education, I am awed by your powers of resistance. I have some knowledge of the attempts that have been made in many classrooms and lecture halls to persuade you that there is little to admire in America. For the second time in this century, capitalism and free enterprise are under assault. Privately owned business is blamed for spoiling the environment, exploiting the worker and seducing, if not outright raping, the customer. Those who make the charge have the solution, of course—government regulation and control. We may never get around to explaining how citizens, who are so gullible that they can be suckered into buying cereal or soap that they don't need and would not be good for them, can at the same time be astute enough to choose representatives in government to which they would entrust the running of their lives.

Not too long ago, a poll was taken on 2,500 college campuses in this country. Thousands and thousands of responses were obtained. Overwhelmingly, sixty-five, seventy, and seventy-five percent of the students found business responsible, as I have said before, for the things that were wrong in this country. That same number said that government was the solution and should take over the management and the control of private business. Eighty percent of the respondents said they wanted government to keep its paws out of their private lives.

We are told every day that the assembly-line worker is becoming a dull-witted robot and that mass production results in standardization. Well, there isn't a socialist country in the world that would not give its copy of Karl Marx for our standardization.

Standardization means production for the masses and the assembly line means more leisure for the worker—freedom from backbreaking and mind-dulling drudgery that man had known for centuries past. Karl Marx did not abolish child labor or free the women from working in the coal mines in England—the steam engine and modern machinery did that.

Unfortunately, the disciples of the new order have had a hand in determining too much policy in recent decades. Government has grown in size and power and cost through the New Deal, the Fair Deal, the New Frontier and the Great Society. It costs more for government today than a family pays for food, shelter and clothing combined. Not even the Office of Management and Budget knows how many boards, commissions, bureaus, and agencies there are in the federal government, but the federal registry, listing their regulations, is just a few pages short of being as big as the Encyclopedia Britannica.

During the Great Society we saw the greatest growth of this government. There were eight Cabinet departments and twelve independent agencies to administer the federal health program. There were thirty-five housing programs and twenty transportation projects. Public utilities had to cope with twenty-seven different agencies on just routine business. There were 192 installations and nine departments with 1,000 projects having to do with the field of pollution.

One congressman found the federal government was spending $4 billion on research in its own laboratories but did not know where they were, how many people were working in them, or what they were doing. One of the research projects was "The Demography of Happiness," and for $249,000 we found that "people who make more money are happier than people who make less, young people are happier than old people, and people who are healthier are happier than people who are sick." For fifteen cents they could have bought an Almanac and read the old bromide, "It's better to be rich, young and healthy than poor, old and sick."

The course that you have chosen is far more in tune with the hopes and aspirations of our people than are those who would sacrifice freedom for some fancied security.

Standing on the tiny deck of the Arabella in 1630 off the Massachusetts coast, John Winthrop said, "We will be as a city upon a hill. The eyes of all people are upon us, so that if we deal falsely with our God in this work we have undertaken and so cause Him to withdraw His present help from us, we shall be made a story and a byword throughout the world." Well, we have not dealt falsely with our God, even if He is temporarily suspended from the classroom.

When I was born, my life expectancy was ten years less than I have already lived—that's a cause of regret for some people in California, I know. Ninety percent of Americans at that time lived beneath what is considered the poverty line today, three-quarters lived in what is considered substandard housing. Today each of those figures is less than ten percent. We have increased our life expectancy by wiping out, almost totally diseases that still ravage mankind in other parts of the world. I doubt if the young people here tonight know the names of some of the diseases that were commonplace when we were growing up. We have more doctors per thousand people than any nation in the world. We have more hospitals that any nation in the world.

When I was your age, believe it or not, none of us knew that we even had a racial problem. When I graduated from college and became a radio sports announcer, broadcasting major league baseball, I didn't have a Hank Aaron or a Willie Mays to talk about. The Spaulding Guide said baseball was a game for Caucasian gentlemen. Some of us then began editorializing and campaigning against this. Gradually we campaigned against all those other areas where the constitutional rights of a large segment of our citizenry were being denied. We have not finished the job. We still have a long way to go, but we have made more progress in a few years than we have made in more than a century.

One-third of all the students in the world who are pursuing higher education are doing so in the United States. The percentage of our young Negro community that is going to college is greater than the percentage of whites in any other country in the world.

One-half of all the economic activity in the entire history of man has taken place in this republic. We have distributed our wealth more widely among our people than any society known to man. Americans work less hours for a higher standard of living than any other people. Ninety-five percent of all our families have an adequate daily intake of nutrients—and a part of the five percent that don't are trying to lose weight! Ninety-nine percent have gas or electric refrigeration, ninety-two percent have televisions, and an equal number have telephones. There are 120 million cars on our streets and highways—and all of them are on the street at once when you are trying to get home at night. But isn't this just proof of our materialism—the very thing that we are charged with? Well, we also have more churches, more libraries, we support voluntarily more symphony orchestras and opera companies, non-profit theaters, and publish more books than all the other nations of the world put together.

Somehow America has bred a kindliness into our people unmatched anywhere, as has been pointed out in that best-selling record by a Canadian journalist. We are not a sick society. A sick society could not produce the men that set foot on the moon, or who are now circling the earth above us in the Skylab. A sick society bereft of morality and courage did not produce the men who went through those year of torture and captivity in Vietnam. Where did we find such men? They are typical of this land, as the Founding Fathers were typical. We found them in our streets, in the offices, the shops and the working places of our country and on the farms.

We cannot escape our destiny, nor should we try to do so. The leadership of the free world was thrust upon us two centuries ago in that little hall of Philadelphia. In the days following World War II, when the economic strength and power of America was all that stood between the world and the return to the dark ages,

Pope Pius XII said, "The American people have a great genius for splendid and unselfish actions. Into the hands of America God has placed the destinies of an afflicted mankind."

We are indeed, and we are today, the last best hope of man on earth.

4

LET THEM GO
THEIR WAY

In the 1974 post-Watergate, mid-term elections, Republicans took heavy losses in Congress, governorship, and legislature. Therefore, some said that the Republications would need a new third party in order to win the White House in '76. But Reagan, along with many other politicians, knew any realignment of the GOP should be done in the context of a two-party system. Reagan's party relied on the Great Communicator to lead the effort; thus, at the second Annual CPAC Conference, all eyes were on him.

This time, Reagan didn't opt for poetic quotes, nostalgic stories, or patriotic rally cries; instead, his speech would be all about business. Rather than a new third party, Reagan would propose taking back the Republican Party. He urged others to join him. And, as for those who would not jump on the bandwagon, he simply said, "Let them go their way."

Second Annual Conservative
Political Action Conference

MARCH 1, 1975

———

Since our last meeting we have been through a disastrous election. It is easy for us to be discouraged, as pundits hail that election as a repudiation of our philosophy and even as a mandate of some kind or other. But the significance of the election was not registered by those who voted, but by those who stayed home. If there was anything like a mandate, it will be found among almost two-thirds of the citizens who refused to participate.

Bitter as it is to accept the results of the November election, we should have reason for some optimism. For many years now we have preached "the gospel," in opposition to the philosophy of so-called liberalism which was, in truth, a call to collectivism.

Now, it is possible we have been persuasive to a greater degree than we had ever realized. Few, if any, Democratic party candidates in the last election ran as liberals. Listening to them, I had the eerie feeling we were hearing reruns of Goldwater speeches. I even thought I heard a few of my own.

Bureaucracy was assailed and fiscal responsibility hailed. Even George McGovern donned sackcloth and ashes and did penance for the good people of South Dakota.

But let's not be so naive as to think we are witnessing a mass conversion to the principles of conservatism. Once sworn into office, the victors reverted to type. In their view, apparently, the ends justified the means.

The "Young Turks" had campaigned against "evil politicians." They turned against committee chairmen of their own party, displaying a taste and talent as cutthroat power politicians quite in contrast to their campaign rhetoric and idealism. Still, we must not forget that they molded their campaigning to fit what even they recognized was the mood of the majority. And we must see to it that the people are reminded of this as they now pursue their ideological goals—and pursue them they will.

I know you are aware of the national polls which show that a greater (and increasing) number of Americans—Republicans, Democrats and independents—classify themselves as "conservatives" than ever before. And a poll of rank-and-file union members reveals dissatisfaction with the amount of power their own leaders have assumed, and a resentment of their use of that power for partisan politics. Would it shock you to know that in that poll sixty-eight percent of rank-and-file union members of this country came out endorsing right-to-work legislation?

These polls give cause for some optimism, but at the same time reveal a confusion that exists and the need for a continued effort to "spread the word."

In another recent survey, of 35,000 college and university students polled, three-fourths blame American business and industry for all of our economic and social ills. The same three-fourths think the answer is more (and virtually complete) regimentation and government control of all phases of business—including the imposition of wage and price controls. Yet eighty percent in the same poll want less government interference in their own lives!

In 1972 the people of this country had a clear-cut choice, based on the issues—to a greater extent than any election in half a century. In overwhelming numbers they ignored party labels, not so much to vote for a man or even a policy as to repudiate a philosophy. In doing so they repudiated that final step into the welfare state—that call for the confiscation and redistribution of their earnings on a scale far greater than what we now have. They repudiated the abandonment of national honor and a weakening of this nation's ability to protect itself.

A study has been made that is so revealing that I'm not surprised it has been ignored by a certain number of political commentators and columnists. The political science department of Georgetown University researched the mandate of the 1972 election and recently presented its findings at a seminar.

Taking several major issues which, incidentally, are still the issues of the day, they polled rank-and-file members of the Democratic Party on their approach to these problems. Then they polled the delegates to the two major national conventions—the leaders of the parties.

They found the delegates to the Republican convention almost identical in their responses to those of the rank-and-file Republicans. Yet the delegates to the Democratic convention were miles apart from the thinking of their own party members.

The mandate of 1972 still exists. The people of America have been confused and disturbed by events since that election, but they hold an unchanged philosophy.

Our task is to make them see that what we represent is identical to their own hopes and dreams of what America can and should be. If there are questions as to whether the principles of conservatism hold up in practice, we have the answers to them. Where conservative principles have been tried, they have worked. Gov. Meldrim Thomson is making them work in New Hampshire; so is Arch Moore in West Virginia and Mills Godwin in Virginia. Jack Williams made them work in Arizona and I'm sure Jim Edwards will in South Carolina.

If you will permit me, I can recount my own experience in California.

When I went to Sacramento eight years ago, I had the belief that government was no deep, dark mystery, that it could be operated efficiently by using the same common sense practiced in our everyday life, in our homes, in business and private affairs.

The "lab test" of my theory—California—was pretty messed up after eight years of a road show version of the Great Society. Our first and only briefing came from the outgoing director of finance, who said: "We're spending $1 million more a day than we're taking in. I have a golf date. Good luck!" That was the most cheerful news we were to hear for quite some time.

California state government was increasing by about 5,000 new employees a year. We were the welfare capital of the world, with sixteen percent of the nation's caseload. Soon California's caseload was increasing by 40,000 a month.

We turned to the people themselves for help. Two hundred fifty experts in the various fields volunteered to serve on task forces at no cost to the taxpayers. They went into every department of state government and came back with 1,800 recommendations on how modern business practices could be used to make government more efficient. We adopted 1,600 of them.

We instituted a policy of "cut, squeeze and trim" and froze the hiring of employees as replacements for retiring employees or others leaving state service.

After a few years of struggling with the professional welfarists, we again turned to the people. First, we obtained another task force and, when the Legislature refused to help implement its recommendations, we presented the recommendations to the electorate.

It still took some doing. The Legislature insisted our reforms would not work, that the needy would starve in the streets, that the workload would be dumped on the counties, that property taxes would go up, and that we'd run up a deficit the first year of $750 million.

That was four years ago. Today, the needy have had an average increase of forty-three percent in welfare grants in California, but the taxpayers have saved $2 billion by the caseload not increasing that 40,000 a month. Instead, there are some 400,000 fewer on welfare today than then.

Forty of the state's fifty-eight counties have reduced property taxes for two years in a row (some for three). That $750 million deficit turned into an $850 million surplus, which we returned to the people in a one-time tax rebate. That wasn't easy. One state senator described that rebate as "an unnecessary expenditure of public funds."

For more than two decades governments—federal, state, local—have been increasing in size two and a half times faster than the population increase. In the last ten years they have increased in cost the payroll seven times as fast as the increase in numbers.

We have just turned over to a new administration in Sacramento, a government virtually the same size it was eight years ago. With the state's growth rate, this means that government absorbed a workload increase, in some departments as much as sixty-six percent.

We also turned over—for the first time in almost a quarter of a century—a balanced budget and a surplus of $500 million. In these eight years just past, we returned to the people in rebates, tax reductions, and bridge toll reductions $5.7 billion. All of this is contrary to the will of those who deplore conservatism and profess to be liberals, yet all of it is pleasing to its citizenry.

Make no mistake; the leadership of the Democratic Party is still out of step with the majority of Americans.

Speaker Carl Albert recently was quoted as saying that our problem is "sixty percent recession, thirty percent inflation and ten percent energy." That makes as much sense as saying two and two make twenty-two.

Without inflation there would be no recession. And unless we curb inflation, we can see the end of our society and economic system. The painful fact is we can only halt inflation by undergoing a period of economic dislocation—a recession, if you will.

We can take steps to ease the suffering of some who will be hurt more than others, but if we turn from fighting inflation and adopt a program only to fight recession, we are on the road to disaster.

In his first address to Congress, the president asked Congress to join him in an all-out effort to balance the budget. I think all of us wish that he had reissued that speech instead of this year's budget message.

What side can be taken in a debate over whether the deficit should be $52 billion or $70 billion or $80 billion preferred by the profligate Congress?

Inflation has one cause and one cause only: government spending more than government takes in. And the cure to inflation is a balanced budget. We know of course, after forty years of social tinkering and Keynesian experimentation, that we can't do this all at once, but it can be achieved. Balancing the budget is like protecting your virtue: you have to learn to say "no."

This is no time to repeat the shopworn panaceas of the New Deal, the Fair Deal, and the Great Society. John Kenneth Galbraith, who, in my opinion, is living proof that economics is an inexact science, has written a new book. It is called *Economics and the Public Purpose*. In it, he asserts that market arrangements in our economy have given us inadequate housing, terrible mass transit, poor healthcare and a host of other miseries. And then, for the first time to my knowledge, he advances socialism as the answer to our problems.

Shorn of all side issues and extraneous matter, the problem underlying all others is the worldwide contest for the hearts and minds of mankind. Do we find the answers to human misery in freedom as it is known, or do we sink into the deadly dullness of the socialist ant heap?

Those who suggest that the latter is some kind of solution are, I think, open to challenge. Let's have no more theorizing when actual comparison is possible. There is in the world a great nation, larger than ours in territory and populated with 250 million capable people. It is rich in resources and has had more than fifty uninterrupted years to practice socialism without opposition.

We could match them, but it would take a little doing on our part. We'd have to cut our paychecks back by seventy-five percent;

move 60 million workers back to the farm; abandon two-thirds of our steel-making capacity; destroy 40 million television sets; tear up fourteen of every fifteen miles of highway; junk nineteen of every twenty automobiles; tear up two-thirds of our railroad tracks; knock down seventy percent of our houses; and rip out nine out of every ten telephones. Then all we have to do is find a capitalist country to sell us wheat on credit to keep us from starving!

Our people are in a time of discontent. Our vital energy supplies are threatened by possibly the most powerful cartel in human history. Our traditional allies in Western Europe are experiencing political and economic instability bordering on chaos.

We seem to be increasingly alone in a world grown more hostile, but we let our defenses shrink to pre-Pearl Harbor levels. And we are conscious that in Moscow the crash buildup of arms continues. The SALT II agreement in Vladivostok, if not renegotiated, guarantees the Soviets a clear missile superiority sufficient to make a "first strike" possible with little fear of reprisal. Yet too many congressmen demand further cuts in our own defenses, including delay, if not cancellation of the B-1 bomber.

I realize that millions of Americans are sick of hearing about Indochina, and perhaps it is politically unwise to talk of our obligation to Cambodia and South Vietnam. But we pledged—in an agreement that brought our men home and freed our prisoners to give our allies arms and ammunition to replace on a one-for-one basis what they expend in resisting the aggression of the Communists who are violating the cease-fire and are fully aided by their Soviet and Red Chinese allies. Congress has already reduced the appropriation to half of what they need and threatens to reduce it even more.

Can we live with ourselves if we, as a nation, betray our friends and ignore our pledged word? And if we do, who would ever trust us again? To consider committing such an act so contrary to our deepest ideals is symptomatic of the erosion of standards and values. And this adds to our discontent.

We did not seek world leadership; it was thrust upon us. It has been our destiny almost from the first moment this land was settled. If we fail to keep our rendezvous with destiny or, as John Winthrop said in 1630, "Deal falsely with our God," we shall be made "a story and byword throughout the world."

Americans are hungry to feel once again a sense of mission and greatness.

I don't know about you, but I am impatient with those Republicans who, after the last election, rushed into print saying, "We must broaden the base of our party," when what they meant was to fuzz up and blur even more the differences between ourselves and our opponents.

It was a feeling that there was not a sufficient difference now between the parties that kept a majority of the voters away from the polls. When have we ever advocated a closed-door policy? Who has ever been barred from participating?

Our people look for a cause to believe in. Is it a third party we need? Or is it a new and revitalized second party, raising a banner of no pale pastels, but bold colors which make it unmistakably clear where we stand on all of the issues troubling the people.

Let us show that we stand for fiscal integrity and sound money and above all for an end to deficit spending, with ultimate retirement of the national debt.

Let us also include a permanent limit on the percentage of the people's earnings government can take without their consent.

Let our banner proclaim a genuine tax reform that will begin by simplifying the income tax so that workers can compute their obligation without having to employ legal help.

And let it provide indexing—adjusting the brackets to the cost of living—so that an increase in salary merely to keep pace with inflation does not move the taxpayer into a surtax bracket. Failure to provide this means an increase in government's share and would make the worker worse off than he was before he got the raise.

Let our banner proclaim our belief in a free market as the greatest provider for the people. Let us also call for an end to the nit-picking, the harassment and overregulation of business and industry which restricts expansion and our ability to compete in world markets.

Let us explore ways to ward off socialism, not by increasing government's coercive power but by increasing participation by the people in the ownership of our industrial machine.

Our banner must recognize the responsibility of government to protect the law-abiding, holding those who commit misdeeds personally accountable.

And we must make it plain to international adventurers that our love of peace stops short of "peace at any price."

We will maintain whatever level of strength is necessary to preserve our free way of life.

A political party cannot be all things to all people. It must represent certain fundamental beliefs, which must not be compromised to political expediency or simply to swell its numbers.

I do not believe I have proposed anything that is contrary to what has been considered Republican principle. It is at the same time the very basis of conservatism. It is time to reassert that principle and raise it to full view. And if there are those who cannot subscribe to these principles, then let them go their way.

5

NO PLACE FOR PALE PASTELS

The GOP took a major hit from the Watergate scandal and President Nixon's resignation. After, Reagan boldly battled incumbent President Gerald Ford for the 1976 Republican nomination, loosing by only a narrow margin.

At the start of his run against Ford, Reagan held close to politics' "eleventh commandment" of GOP etiquette: Thou shalt not speak ill of any fellow Republican. But as campaign debt and primary losses mounted, his cohorts began advising the Gipper otherwise. Soon, his speeches took a negative turn, underscoring Ford's policy of détente with the Soviets, especially the incumbent's proposal to "give away" the Panama Canal to our Cold War adversaries.

Despite Reagan's harsh criticisms of his opponent, Ford graciously invited him on stage to address the crowd. In an impromptu speech, Reagan glowed, even in defeat, galvanizing the crowd before him. The reaction of the crowd proved Reagan a president-in-waiting—a reality that rested only four short years ahead.

Republican National Convention, Kansas City, Missouri

AUGUST 19, 1976

———

Mr. President, Mrs. Ford, Mr. Vice President, Mr. Vice President-to-be, the distinguished guests here, and you, ladies and gentlemen. I'm going to say fellow Republicans here, but those who are watching from a distance, with all those millions of Democrats and Independents who I know are looking for a cause around which to rally and which I believe we can give them:

There are cynics who say that a party platform is something no one bothers to read and doesn't very often amount to much. Whether it is different this time than it has ever been before, I believe the Republican Party has a platform that is a banner of bold, unmistakable colors with no pale, pastel shades.

We have just heard a call to arms based on that platform, and a call to us to really be successful in communicating and reveal to the American people the difference between this platform and the platform of the opposing party, which is nothing but revamp and a reissue and a running of the late, late show of the thing that we've been hearing from them for the last forty years.

If I could just take a moment. I had an assignment the other day. Someone asked me to write a letter for a time capsule that is going to be opened in Los Angeles a hundred years from now, on our tercentennial. It sounded like an easy assignment. They suggested I write something about the problems and issues of the day, and I set out to do so, riding down the coast in an automobile looking at the blue Pacific out on one side and the Santa Ynez mountains on the other, and I couldn't help but wonder if it was going to be that beautiful a hundred years from now as it was on that summer day.

And then, as I tried to write—let your own minds turn to that task. You're going to write for people a hundred years from now who know all about us. We know nothing about them. We don't know what kind of a world they'll be living in.

And suddenly I thought to myself, if I write of problems they'll be domestic problems, of which the president spoke here tonight, the challenges confronting us, erosion of freedom that has taken place under Democratic rule in this country, the invasion of private rights, the controls and restrictions on the vitality of the great free economy that we enjoy. These are the challenges that we must meet.

And then again there is the challenge of which he spoke, that we live in a world in which the great powers have poised and aimed at each other horrible missiles of destruction that can, in a matter of minutes, arrive in each other's country and destroy virtually the civilized world we live in.

And suddenly it dawned on me.

Those who would read this letter a hundred years from now will know whether those missiles were fired. They will know whether we met our challenge. Whether they have the freedoms that we have known up until now will depend on what we do here.

Will they look back with appreciation and say, "Thank God for those people in 1976 who headed off that loss of freedom, who kept our world from nuclear destruction"?

And if we fail, they probably won't get to read the letter at all, because it spoke of individual freedom and they won't be allowed to talk of that or read of it.

This is our challenge. And this is why, here in this hall tonight, better than we've ever done before, we have got to quit talking to each other and about each other, and go out and communicate to the world that we may be fewer in numbers than we've ever been but we carry the message they're waiting for.

We must go forth from here united, determined that what a great general said a few years ago is true: "There's no substitute for victory."

6

THE NEW
REPUBLICAN PARTY

Once Jimmy Carter defeated Gerald Ford in the 1976 presidential race, Reagan was more in-spired than ever to bring Americans together. He knew that the Republican base needed to be broadened if there was any chance of him reaching the White House in 1980. Speaking only a few weeks after Carter took his oath of office, Reagan once again graced CPAC, this time at its fourth annual convention.

Reagan would rally a new conservative backing by recalling the constitutional principles that guided our nation, and still do. He would concentrate his efforts in the same way that President Lincoln had: by working to win the black vote. Furthermore, to be successful, Reagan knew it was time he captured as much of the Democratic vote as possible–a goal he addressed time and again in his rhetoric of the 1970s..

Fourth Annual Conservative
Political Action Conference

FEBRUARY 6, 1977

———

I'm happy to be back with you in this annual event after missing last year's meeting. I had some business in New Hampshire that wouldn't wait.

Three weeks ago, here in our nation's capital, I told a group of conservative scholars that we are currently in the midst of a reordering of the political realities that have shaped our time. We know today that the principles and values that lie at the heart of conservatism are shared by the majority.

Despite what some in the press may say, we who are proud to call ourselves "conservative" are not a minority of a minority party; we are part of the great majority of Americans of both major parties and of most of the independents as well.

A Harris poll released September 7, 1975, showed eighteen percent identifying themselves as liberal and thirty-one percent as conservative, with forty-one percent as middle of the road; a few months later, on January 5, 1976, by a 43-19 plurality those polled by Harris said they would "prefer to see the country move in a more conservative direction than a liberal one."

Last October 24, the Gallup organization released the result of a poll taken right in the midst of the presidential campaign.

Respondents were asked to state where they would place themselves on a scale ranging from "right-of-center" (which was defined as "conservative") to "left-of-center" (which was defined as "liberal").

- Thirty-seven percent viewed themselves as left-of-center or liberal

- Twelve percent placed themselves in the middle

- Fifty-one percent said they were right-of-center, that is, conservative.

What I find interesting about this particular poll is that it offered those polled a range of choices on a left-right continuum. This seems to me to be a more realistic approach than dividing the world into strict left and rights. Most of us, I guess, like to think of ourselves as avoiding both extremes, and the fact that a majority of Americans chose one or the other position on the right end of the spectrum is really impressive.

Those polls confirm that most Americans are basically conservative in their outlook. But once we have said this, we conservatives have not solved our problems; we have merely stated them clearly. Yes, conservatism can and does mean different things to those who call themselves conservatives.

You know, as I do, that most commentators make a distinction between what they call "social" conservatism and "economic" conservatism. The so-called social issues—law and order, abortion, busing, quota systems—are usually associated with blue-collar, ethnic and religious groups themselves traditionally associated with the Democratic Party. The economic issues—inflation, deficit spending, and big government—are usually associated with Republican Party members and independents, who concentrate their attention on economic matters.

Now, I am willing to accept this view of two major kinds of conservatism—or, better still, two different conservative constituencies. But at the same time let me say that the old lines that once clearly divided these two kinds of conservatism are disappearing.

In fact, the time has come to see if it is possible to present a program of action based on political principle that can attract those interested in the so-called social issues and those interested in "economic" issues. In short, isn't it possible to combine the two major segments of contemporary American conservatism into one politically effective whole?

I believe the answer is yes, it is possible to create a political entity that will reflect the views of the great, hitherto conservative, majority. We went a long way toward doing it in California. We can do it in America. This is not a dream, a wistful hope. It is and has been a reality. I have seen the conservative future and it works.

Let me say again what I said to our conservative friends from the academic world: What I envision is not simply a melding together of the two branches of American conservatism into a temporary uneasy alliance, but the creation of a new, lasting majority.

This will mean compromise. But not a compromise of basic principle. What will emerge will be something new—something open and vital and dynamic, something the great conservative majority will recognize as its own, because at the heart of this undertaking is principled politics.

I have always been puzzled by the inability of some political and media types to understand exactly what is meant by adherence to political principle. All too often in the press and the television evening news it is treated as a call for "ideological purity." Whatever ideology may mean—and it seems to mean a variety of things, depending upon who is using it—it always conjures up in my mind a picture of a rigid, irrational clinging to abstract theory in the face of reality. We have to recognize that in this country "ideology" is a scare word. And for good reason. Marxist-Leninism is, to give but one example, an ideology. All the facts of the real world have to be fitted to the Procrustean bed of Marx and Lenin. If the facts don't happen to fit the ideology, the facts are chopped off and discarded.

I consider this to be the complete opposite to principled conservatism. If there is any political viewpoint in this world which is free from slavish adherence to abstraction, it is American conservatism.

When a conservative states that the free market is the best mechanism ever devised by the mind of man to meet material needs, he is merely stating what a careful examination of the real world has told him is the truth.

When a conservative says that totalitarian Communism is an absolute enemy of human freedom, he is not theorizing—he is reporting the ugly reality captured so unforgettably in the writings of Alexander Solzhenitsyn.

When a conservative says it is bad for the government to spend more than it takes in, he is simply showing the same common sense that tells him to come in out of the rain.

When a conservative says that busing does not work, he is not appealing to some theory of education—he is merely reporting what he has seen down at the local school.

When a conservative quotes Jefferson that government that is closest to the people is best, it is because he knows that Jefferson risked his life, his fortune and his sacred honor to make certain that what he and his fellow patriots learned from experience was not crushed by an ideology of empire.

Conservatism is the antithesis of the kind of ideological fanaticism that has brought so much horror and destruction to the world. The common sense and common decency of ordinary men and women, working out their own lives in their own way—this is the heart of American conservatism today. Conservative wisdom and principles are derived from willingness to learn, not just from what is going on now, but from what has happened before.

The principles of conservatism are sound because they are based on what men and women have discovered through experience in not just one generation or a dozen, but in all the combined experience of mankind. When we conservatives say that we know something about political affairs and that what we know can be stated as principles, we are saying that the principles we hold dear are those that have been found, through experience, to be ultimately beneficial for individuals, for families, for communities and for nations—found through the often bitter testing of pain, or sacrifice and sorrow.

One thing that must be made clear in post-Watergate is this: The American new conservative majority we represent is not based on abstract theorizing of the kind that turns off the American people, but on common sense, intelligence, reason, hard work, faith in God, and the guts to say, "Yes, there are things we do strongly believe in that we are willing to live for, and yes, if necessary, to die for." That is not "ideological purity." It is simply what built this country and kept it great.

Let us lay to rest, once and for all, the myth of a small group of ideological purists trying to capture a majority. Replace it with the reality of a majority trying to assert its rights against the tyranny of powerful academics, fashionable left-revolutionaries, some economic illiterates who happen to hold elective office, and the social engineers who dominate the dialogue and set the format in political and social affairs.

If there is any ideological fanaticism in American political life, it is to be found among the enemies of freedom on the left or right—those who would sacrifice principle to theory, those who worship only the god of political, social and economic abstractions, ignoring the realities of everyday life. They are not conservatives.

Our first job is to get this message across to those who share most of our principles. If we allow ourselves to be portrayed as ideological shock troops without correcting this error, we are doing ourselves and our cause a disservice. Wherever and whenever we can, we should gently but firmly correct our political and media friends who have been perpetuating the myth of conservatism as a narrow ideology. Whatever the word may have meant in the past, today conservatism means principles evolving from experience and a belief in change when necessary, but not just for the sake of change.

One we have established this, the next question is: What will be the political vehicle by which the majority can assert its rights?

I have to say I cannot agree with some of my friends—perhaps including some of you here tonight—who have answered that question by saying this nation needs a new political party.

I respect that view and I know that those who have reached it have done so after long hours of study. But I believe that political success of the principles we believe in can best be achieved in the Republican Party. I believe the Republican Party can hold and should provide the political mechanism through which the goals of the majority of Americans can be achieved. For one thing, the biggest single grouping of conservatives is to be found in that party. It makes more sense to build on that grouping than to break it up and start over. Rather than a third party, we can have a new first party made up of people who share our principles. I have said before that if a formal change in name proves desirable, then so be it. But tonight, for purpose of discussion, I'm going to refer it simply as the New Republican Party.

And let me say so there can be no mistakes as to what I mean: The New Republican Party I envision will not be, and cannot be, one limited to the country club-big business image that, for reasons both fair and unfair, it is burdened with today. The New Republican Party I am speaking about is going to have room for the man and the woman in the factories, for the farmer, for the cop on the beat, and the millions of Americans who may never have thought of joining our party before, but whose interests coincide with those represented by principled Republicanism.

If we are to attract more working men and women of this country, we will do so not by simply "making room" for them, but by making certain they have a say in what goes on in the party. The Democratic Party turned its back on the majority of social conservatives during the 1960s. The New Republican Party of the late seventies and eighties must welcome them, seek them out, enlist them, not only as rank-and-file members but as leaders and as candidates.

The time has come for Republicans to say to black voters: "Look, we offer principles that black Americans can, and do, support. We believe in jobs, real jobs; we believe in education that is really education; we believe in treating all Americans as individuals and not as stereotypes or voting blocs—and we believe that the long-range interest of black Americans lies in looking at what each major party has to offer and then deciding on the merits." The Democratic Party takes the black vote for granted. Well, it's time black America and the New Republican Party move toward each other and create a situation in which no black vote can be taken for granted.

The New Republican Party I envision is one that will energetically seek out the best candidates for every elective office, candidates who not only agree with, but understand and are willing to fight for, a sound, honest economy, for the interests of American families and neighborhoods and communities and a strong national defense. And these candidates must be able to communicate those principles to the American people in language they understand. Inflation isn't a textbook problem. Unemployment isn't a textbook problem. They should be discussed in human terms.

Our candidates must be willing to communicate with every level of society, because the principles we espouse are universal and cut across traditional lines. In every congressional district there should be a search made for young men and women who share these principles, and they should be brought into positions of leadership in the local Republican Party groups. We can find attractive, articulate candidates if we look, and when we find them, we will begin to change the sorry state of affairs that has led to a Democratic-controlled Congress for more than forty years.

I need not remind you that you can have the soundest principles in the world, but if you don't have candidates who can communicate those principles, candidates who are articulate as well as principled, you are going to lose election after election. I refuse to believe that the good Lord divided this world into Republicans who defend basic values and Democrats who win elections. We have to find tough, bright young men and women who are sick and tired of clichés and the pomposity and the mind-numbing economic idiocy of the liberals in Washington.

It is at this point, however, that we come across a question that is really the essential one: What will be the basis of this New Republican Party? To what set of values and principles can our candidates appeal? Where can Americans who want to know where we stand look for guidance?

Fortunately, we have an answer to that question. That answer was provided last summer by the men and women of the Republican Party—not just the leadership, but the ones who have built the party on local levels all across the country.

The answer was provided in the 1976 platform of the Republican Party.

This was not a document handed down from on high. It was hammered out in free and open debate among all those who care about our party and the principles it stands for.

The Republican platform is unique. Unlike any other party platform I have ever seen, it answers not only programmatic questions for the immediate future of the party, but also provides a clear outline of the underlying principles upon which those programs are based.

The New Republican Party can and should use the Republican platform of 1976 as the major source from which a Declaration of Principles can be created and offered to the American people.

Tonight I want to offer to you my own version of what such a declaration might look like. I make no claim to originality. This declaration I propose is relatively short, taken, for most part, word for word from the Republican platform. It concerns itself with basic principles, not with specific solutions.

We, the members of the New Republican Party, believe that the preservation and enhancement of the values that strengthen and protect individual freedom, family life, communities and neighborhoods and the liberty of our beloved nation should be at the heart of any legislative or political program presented to the American people. Toward that end, we therefore commit ourselves to the following propositions and offer them to each American believing that the New Republican Party, based on such principles, will serve the interests of all the American people.

We believe that liberty can be measured by how much freedom Americans have to make their own decisions, even their own mistakes. Government must step in when one's liberties impinge on one's neighbors. Government must protect constitutional rights, deal with other governments, protect citizens from aggressors, assure equal opportunity, and be compassionate in caring for those citizens who are unable to care for themselves.

Our federal system of local-state-national government is designed to sort out on what level these actions should be taken. Those concerns of a national character—such as air and water pollution that do not respect state boundaries, or the national transportation system, or efforts to safeguard your civil liberties—must, of course, be handled on the national level.

As a general rule, however, we believe that government action should be taken first by the government that resides as close to you as possible.

We also believe that Americans, often acting through voluntary organizations, should have the opportunity to solve many of the social problems of their communities. This spirit of freely helping others is uniquely American and should be encouraged in every way by government.

Families must continue to be the foundation of our nation.

Families—not government programs—are the best way to make sure our children are properly nurtured, our elderly are cared for, our cultural and spiritual heritages are perpetuated, our laws are observed, and our values are preserved.

Thus it is imperative that our government's programs, actions, officials and social welfare institutions never be allowed to jeopardize the family. We fear the government may be powerful enough to destroy our families; we know that it is not powerful enough to replace them. The New Republican Party must be committed to working always in the interest of the American family.

Every dollar spent by government is a dollar earned by individuals. Government must always ask: Are your dollars being wisely spent? Can we afford it? Is it not better for the country to leave your dollars in your pocket?

Elected officials, their appointees, and government workers are expected to perform their public acts with honesty, openness, diligence and special integrity.

Government must work for the goal of justice and the elimination of unfair practices, but no government has yet designed a more productive economic system or one which benefits as many people as the American market system.

The beauty of our land is our legacy to our children. It must be protected by us so that they can pass it on intact to their children.

The United States must always stand for peace and liberty in the world and the rights of the individual. We must form sturdy partnerships with our allies for the preservation of freedom. We must be ever willing to negotiate differences, but equally mindful that there are American ideals that cannot be compromised. Given that there are other nations with potentially hostile design, we recognize that we can reach our goals only while maintaining a superior national defense, second to none.

In his inaugural speech President Carter said that he saw the world "dominated by a new spirit." He said, and I quote, "The passion for freedom is on the rise."

Well, I don't know how he knows this, but if it is true, then it is the most unrequited passion in human history. The world is being dominated by a new spirit, all right, but it isn't the spirit of freedom.

It isn't very often you see a familiar object that shocks and frightens you. But the other day I came across a map of the world created by Freedom House, an organization monitoring the state of freedom in the world for the past twenty-five years. It is an ordinary map, with one exception: it shows the world's nations in white for free, shaded for partly free and black for not free.

Almost all of the great Eurasian land mass is completely colored black, from the western border of East Germany, through middle and eastern Europe, through the awesome spaces of the Soviet Union, on to the Bering Strait in the north, down past the immensity of China, still further down to Vietnam and the South China Sea—in all that huge, sprawling, inconceivably immense area not a single political or personal or religious freedom exists.

The entire continent of Africa, from the Mediterranean to the Cape of Good Hope, from the Atlantic to the Indian Ocean, all that vastness is almost totally un-free. In the tiny nation of Tanzania alone, according to a report in *The New York Times*, there are 3,000 people in detention for political crimes—that is more than the total being held in South Africa! The Mideast has only one free state: Israel. If a visitor from another planet were to approach earth, and if this planet showed free nations in light and unfree nations in darkness, the pitifully small beacons of light would make him wonder what was hidden in that terrifying, enormous blackness.

We know what is hidden. Gulag. Torture. Families—and human beings—broken apart. No free press, no freedom of religion. The ancient forms of tyranny revived and made even more hideous and strong through what Winston Churchill once called "a perverted science." Men rotting for years in solitary confinement because they have different political and economic beliefs, solitary confinement that drives the fortunate ones insane and makes the survivors wish for death.

Only now and then do we in the West hear a voice from out of that darkness. Then there is silence—the silence of human slavery. There is no more terrifying sound in human experience, with one possible exception. Look at that map again. The very heart of the darkness is the Soviet Union and from that heart comes a different sound. It is the whirring sound of machinery and the whisper of the computer technology we ourselves have sold them. It is the sound of building, building of the strongest military machine ever devised by man. Our military strategy is designed to hopefully prevent a war. Theirs is designed to win one. A group of eminent scientists, scholars, and intelligence experts offer a survey showing that the Soviet Union is driving for military superiority and are derided as hysterically making, quote, "a worst case," unquote, concerning Soviet intentions and capabilities.

But is it not precisely the duty of the national government to be prepared for the worst case? Two senators, after studying the North Atlantic Treaty Organization, have reported to the Armed Forces committee that Soviet forces in Eastern Europe have the capability to launch, with little warning, a "potentially devastating" attack in Central Europe from what is termed a "standing alert."

Reading their report, one can almost see the enormous weight of the parts of the earth that are under tyranny shifting in an irresistible tilt toward that tiny portion of land in freedom's light. Even now in Western Europe we have Communists in the government of Italy, France appeasing terrorists, and England—for centuries the model for the sword of freedom in Western Europe—weak, dispirited, turning inward.

A "worst case"? How could you make a good case out of the facts as they are known? The Soviet Union, poised on the edge of Free Europe, capable of striking from a standing start, has modern tanks in far greater numbers than the outmoded vehicles of NATO. We have taken comfort from NATO's superiority in the air, but now the Soviet Union has made a dramatic swing away from its historic defensive air posture to one capable of support-ing offensive action. NATO's southern flank is described in the Senate report with a single word: shambles.

The report is simply reality as it was, with different names and faces, in Europe in the late 1930s when so many refused to believe and thought if we don't look the threat will go away.

We don't want hysteria. We don't want distortion of Soviet power. We want truth. And above all, we want peace. And to have that, the United States has to immediately reexamine its entire view of the world and develop a strategy of freedom. We cannot be the second-best superpower for the simple reason that he who is second is last. In this deadly game, there are no silver medals for second.

President Carter, as a candidate, said he would cut $5 to $7 billion from the defense budget. We must let him know that while we agree, there must be no fat in our armed forces. Those armed forces must be capable of coping with the new reality presented to us by the Russians, and cutting $7 billion out of our defense budget is not the way to accomplish this. Some years ago, a young president said we will make any sacrifice, bear any burden—and we will, to preserve our freedom.

Our relationship with mainland China is clouded. The so-called "gang of four" are up one day and down the next, and we are seeing the pitfalls of making deals with charismatic personal-ities and living legends. The charisma fades as the living legends die, and those who take their place are interested not in our best wishes but in power. The key word for China today is turmoil. We should watch and observe and analyze as closely and rationally as we can.

But in our relationships with the mainland of China we should always remember that the conditions and possibilities for, and the realities of, freedom exist to an infinitely greater degree with our Chinese friends in Taiwan. We can never go wrong if we do what is morally right, and the moral way—the honorable way—is to keep our commitment, our solemn promise to the people of Taiwan.

Our liberal friends have made much of the lack of freedom in some Latin American countries. Senator Edward Kennedy and his colleagues here in Washington let no opportunity pass to let us know about horrors in Chile. Well, I think when the United States of America is considering a deal with a country that hasn't had an election in almost eight years, where the press is under the thumb of a dictatorship, where ordinary citizens are abducted in the night by secret police, where military domination of the country is known to be harsh on dissenters, and when these things are documented, we should reject overtures from those who rule such a country.

But the country I'm describing is not Chile—it is Panama.

We are negotiating with a dictatorship that comes within the portion of that map colored black for no freedom. No civil rights. One-man rule. No free press.

Candidate Carter said he would never relinquish "actual control" of the Panama Canal. President Carter is negotiating with a dictatorship whose record on civil and human rights is as I have just described, and the negotiations concern the rights guaranteed to us by treaty which we will give up under a threat of violence. In only a few weeks we will mark the second anniversary of the death of freedom for the Vietnamese. An estimated 300,000 of them are being "re-educated" in concentration camps to forget about freedom.

There is only one major question on the agenda of national priorities and that is the state of our national security. I refer, of course, to the state of our armed forces—but also to our state of mind, to the way we perceive the world. We cannot maintain the strength we need to survive, no matter how many missiles we have, no matter how many tanks we build, unless we are willing to reverse the trend of deteriorating faith in and continuing abuse of our national intelligence agencies. Let's stop the sniping and the propaganda and the historical revisionism and let the CIA and the other intelligence agencies do their job!

Let us reverse the trend of public indifference to problems of national security. In every congressional district citizens should join together, enlist and educate neighbors and make certain that congressmen know we care. The front pages of major newspapers on the East Coast recently headlined and told in great detail of a takeover—the takeover of a magazine published in New York, not a nation losing its freedom. You would think, from the attention it received in the media, that it was a matter of blazing national interest whether the magazine lived or died. The tendency of much of the media to ignore the state of our national security is too well documented for me to go on.

My friends, the time has come to start acting to bring about the great conservative majority party we know is waiting to be created.

And just to set the record straight, let me say this about our friends who are now Republicans but who do not identify themselves as conservatives. I want the record to show that I do not view the new revitalized Republican Party as one based on a principle of exclusion. After all, you do not get to be a majority party by searching for groups you won't associate or work with. If we truly believe in our principles, we should sit down and talk. Talk with anyone, anywhere, at any time if it means talking about the principles for the Republican Party. Conservatism is not a narrow ideology, nor is it the exclusive property of conservative activists.

We've succeeded better than we know. Little more than a decade ago more than two-thirds of Americans believed the federal government could solve all our problems and do so without restricting our freedom or bankrupting the nation.

We warned of things to come, of the danger inherent in unwarranted government involvement in things not its proper province. What we warned against has come to pass. And today, more than two-thirds of our citizens are telling us, and each other, that social engineering by the federal government has failed. The Great Society is great only in power, in size and in cost. And so are the problems it set out to solve. Freedom has been diminished, and we stand on the brink of economic ruin.

Our task now is not to sell a philosophy, but to make the majority of Americans, who already share that philosophy, see that modern conservatism offers them a political home. We are not a cult, we are members of a majority. Let's act and talk like it.

The job is ours and the job must be done. If not by us, who? If not now, when?

Our party must be the party of the individual. It must not sell out the individual to cater to the group. No greater challenge faces our society today than ensuring that each one of us can maintain his dignity and his identity in an increasingly complex, centralized society.

Extreme taxation, excessive controls, oppressive government competition with business, galloping inflation, frustrated minorities, and forgotten Americans are not the products of free enterprise. They are the residue of centralized bureaucracy, of government by a self-anointed elite.

Our party must be based on the kind of leadership that grows and takes its strength from the people. Any organization is in actuality only the lengthened shadow of its members. A political party is a mechanical structure created to further a cause. The cause, not the mechanism, brings and holds the members together. And our cause must be to rediscover, reassert, and reapply America's spiritual heritage to our national affairs.

Then, with God's help, we shall indeed be as a city upon a hill, with the eyes of all people upon us.

7

PRESIDENTIAL NOMINATION ACCEPTANCE SPEECH

When Reagan made his second bid for the presidency, the U.S. was in the thick of the Iran Hostage Crisis–a 444-day event that would shake the nation. With each passing day, Carter's administration was criticized for its flimsy foreign policy and overall weak response to the crisis.

Dissatisfaction with the administration led to the emergence of a broad array of Republication candidates. As lesser challengers fell to the fray, New Hampshire's *Nashua Telegraph* newspaper offered to host a debate between Reagan and George H. W. Bush. Reagan, concerned that a newspaper-sponsor wasn't permitted by electoral rules, decided to not only fund the debate himself, but to invite the full group of candidates to participate. But learning about Reagan's decision as the debate was about to commence, an angry George Bush refused to take part. At that, the soundman excitedly decided to mute Reagan's microphone. Noticeably perturbed, Reagan sternly remarked, "I am paying for this microphone, Mr. Green!"

The debate, in the end, did take place between Reagan and Bush alone. The Republicans nominated Reagan and the "microphone" quote lived in infamy.

Republican National Convention, Detroit, Michigan

JULY 17, 1980

Thank you very much. We're using up prime time. Thank you very much.

You're singing our song. Well, the first thrill tonight was to find myself for the first time in a long time in a movie on prime time.

But this, as you can imagine, is the second big thrill.

Mr. Chairman, Mr. Vice President-to-be, this convention, my fellow citizens of this great nation:

With a deep awareness of the responsibility conferred by your trust, I accept your nomination for the presidency of the United States. I do so with deep gratitude. And I think also I might interject on behalf of all of us our thanks to Detroit and the people of Michigan and to this city for the warm hospitality we've enjoyed. And I thank you for your wholehearted response to my recommendation in regard to George Bush as the candidate for vice president.

I'm very proud of our party tonight. This convention has shown to all America a party united, with positive programs for solving the nation's problems, a party ready to build a new consensus with all those across the land who share a community of values embodied in these words: family, work, neighborhood, peace and freedom.

Now, I know we've had a quarrel or two, but only as to the method of attaining a goal. There was no argument here about the goal. As president, I will establish a liaison with the fifty governors to encourage them to eliminate, wherever it exists, discrimination against women. I will monitor federal laws to insure their implementation and to add statutes if they are needed.

More than anything else, I want my candidacy to unify our country, to renew the American spirit and sense of purpose. I want to carry our message to every American, regardless of party affiliation, who is a member of this community of shared values.

Never before in our history have Americans been called upon to face three grave threats to our very existence, any one of which could destroy us. We face a disintegrating economy, a weakened defense, and an energy policy based on the sharing of scarcity.

The major issue in this campaign is the direct political, personal, and moral responsibility of Democratic Party leadership—in the White House and in the Congress—for this unprecedented calamity, which has befallen us. They tell us they've done the most that humanly could be done. They say that the United States has had its day in the sun, that our nation has passed its zenith. They expect you to tell your children that the American people no longer have the will to cope with their problems, that the future will be one of sacrifice and few opportunities.

My fellow citizens, I utterly reject that view. The American people, the most generous on earth, who created the highest standard of living, are not going to accept the notion that we can only make a better world for others by moving backward ourselves. And those who believe we can have no business leading this nation.

I will not stand by and watch this great country destroy itself under mediocre leadership that drifts from one crisis to the next, eroding our national will and purpose. We have come together here because the American people deserve better from those to whom they entrust our nation's highest offices, and we stand united in our resolve to do something about it.

We need a rebirth of the American tradition of leadership at every level of government and in private life as well. The United States of America is unique in world history because it has a genius for leaders—many leaders, on many levels. But back in

1976, Mr. Carter said, "Trust me." And a lot of people did. And now, many of those people are out of work. Many have seen their savings eaten away by inflation. Many others on fixed incomes, especially the elderly, have watched helplessly as the cruel tax of inflation wasted away their purchasing power. And today, a great many who trusted Mr. Carter wonder if we can survive the Carter policies of national defense.

"Trust me" government asks that we concentrate our hopes and dreams on one man, that we trust him to do what's best for us. But my view of government places trust not in one person or one party, but in those values that transcend persons and parties. The trust is where it belongs—in the people. The responsibility to live up to that trust is where it belongs, in their elected leaders. That kind of relationship, between the people and their elected leaders, is a special kind of compact.

Three hundred sixty years ago, in 1620, a group of families dared to cross a mighty ocean to build a future for themselves in a new world. When they arrived at Plymouth, Massachusetts, they formed what they called a "compact," an agreement among themselves to build a community and abide by its laws.

This single act—the voluntary binding together of free people to live under the law—set the pattern for what was to come.

A century and a half later, the descendants of those people pledged their lives, their fortunes and their sacred honor to found this nation. Some forfeited their fortunes and their lives; none sacrificed honor.

Four score and seven years later, Abraham Lincoln called upon the people of all America to renew their dedication and their commitment to a government of, for, and by the people.

Isn't it once again time to renew our compact of freedom—to pledge to each other all that is best in our lives, all that gives meaning to them, for the sake of this, our beloved and blessed land?

Together, let us make this a new beginning. Let us make a commitment to care for the needy; to teach our children the values handed down to us by our families; to have the courage to defend those values and virtues and the willingness to sacrifice for them.

Let us pledge to restore, in our time, the American spirit of voluntary service, of cooperation, of private and community initiative—a spirit that flows like a deep and mighty river through the history of our nation.

As your nominee, I pledge to you to restore to the federal government the capacity to do the people's work without dominating their lives. I pledge to you a government that will not only work well but wisely, its ability to act tempered by prudence and its willingness to do good balanced by the knowledge that government is never more dangerous than when our desire to have it help us blinds us to its great power to harm us.

You know, the first Republican president once said, "While the people retain their virtue and their vigilance, no administration by any extreme of wickedness or folly can seriously injure the government in the short space of four years." If Mr. Lincoln could see what's happened in these last three and a half years, he might hedge a little on that statement. But with the virtues that are our legacy as a free people and with the vigilance that sustains liberty, we still have time to use our renewed compact to overcome the injuries that have been done to America these past three and a half years.

First, we must overcome something the present administration has cooked up: a new and altogether indigestible economic stew, one part inflation, one part high unemployment, one part recession, one part runaway taxes, one part deficit spending, seasoned with an energy crisis. It's an economic stew that has turned the national stomach.

Ours are not problems of abstract economic theory. These are problems of flesh and blood, problems that cause pain and destroy the moral fiber of real people who should not suffer the further indignity of being told by the government that it is all somehow their fault. We do not have inflation because—as Mr. Carter says—we've lived too well.

The head of a government which has utterly refused to live within its means and which has, in the last few days, told us that this coming year's deficit will be $60 billion, dares to point the finger of blame at business and labor, both of which have been engaged in a losing struggle just trying to stay even.

High taxes, we are told, are somehow good for us—as if, when government spends our money, it isn't inflationary; but when we spend it, it is.

Those who preside over the worst energy shortage in our history tell us to use less so that we will run out of oil, gasoline, and natural gas a little more slowly. Well, now, conservation is desirable, of course; we must not waste energy. But conservation is not the sole answer to our energy needs.

America must get to work producing more energy. The Republican program for solving economic problems is based on growth and productivity.

Large amounts of oil and natural gas lie beneath our land and off our shores, untouched because the present administration seems to believe the American people would rather see more regulation, more taxes, and more controls than more energy.

Coal offers a great potential. So does nuclear energy, produced under rigorous safety standards. It could supply electricity for thousands of industries and millions of jobs and homes. It must not be thwarted by a tiny minority opposed to economic growth, which often finds friendly ears in regulatory agencies for its obstructionist campaigns.

Now, make no mistake. We will not permit the safety of our people or our environmental heritage to be jeopardized, but we are going to reaffirm that the economic prosperity of our people is a fundamental part of our environment. Our problems are both acute and chronic, yet all we hear from those in positions of leadership are the same tired proposals for more government tinkering, more meddling and more control—all of which led us to this sorry state in the first place.

Can anyone look at the record of this administration and say, "Well done"? Can anyone compare the state of our economy when the Carter administration took office with where we are today and say, "Keep up the good work"? Can anyone look at our reduced standing in the world today and say, "Let's have four more years of this"?

I believe the American people are going to answer these questions, as you've answered them, in the first week of November and their answer will be, "No! We've had enough." And then it will be up to us—beginning next January 20—to offer an administration and congressional leadership of competence and more than a little courage.

We must have the clarity of vision to see the difference between what is essential and what is merely desirable, and then the courage to bring our government back under control.

It is essential that we maintain both the forward momentum of economic growth and the strength of the safety net beneath those in our society who need help. We also believe it is essential that the integrity of all aspects of Social Security be preserved.

Beyond these essentials, I believe it is clear our federal government is overgrown and overweight. Indeed, it is time our government should go on a diet. Therefore, my first act as chief executive will be to impose an immediate and thorough freeze on federal hiring. Then we are going to enlist the very best minds from business, labor, and whatever quarter to conduct a detailed review of every department, bureau, and agency that lives by federal appropriation.

And we are also going to enlist the help and ideas of many dedicated and hard-working government employees at all levels who want a more efficient government just as much as the rest of us do. I know that many of them are demoralized by the confusion and waste they confront in their work as a result of failed and failing policies.

Our instructions to the groups we enlist will be simple and direct. We will remind them that government programs exist at the sufferance of the American taxpayer and are paid for with money earned by working men and women, and programs that represent a waste of their money—a theft from their pocket-books—must have that waste eliminated or that program must go. It must go by executive order where possible, by congressional action where necessary.

Everything that can be run more effectively by state and local government we shall turn over to state and local government, along with the funding sources to pay for it. We are going to put an end to the money merry-go-round, where our money becomes Washington's money, to be spent by states and cities exactly the way the federal bureaucrats tell us it has to be spent.

I will not accept the excuse that the federal government has grown so big and powerful that it is beyond the control of any president, any administration, or Congress. We are going to put an end to the notion that the American taxpayer exists to fund the federal government. The federal government exists to serve the American people and to be accountable to the American people. On January 20, we are going to reestablish that truth.

Also on that date, we are going to initiate action to get substantial relief for our taxpaying citizens and action to put people back to work. None of this will be based on any new form of monetary tinkering or fiscal sleight of hand. We will simply apply to government the common sense that we all use in our daily lives.

Work and family are at the center of our lives, the foundation of our dignity as a free people. When we deprive people of what they have earned or take away their jobs, we destroy their dignity and undermine their families. We can't support families unless there are jobs; and we can't have jobs unless the people have both money to invest and the faith to invest it.

These are concepts that stem from an economic system that for more than two hundred years has helped us master a continent, create a previously undreamed-of prosperity for our people, and feed millions of others around the globe, and that system will

continue to serve us in the future if our government will stop ignoring the basic values on which it was built and stop betraying
the trust and good will of the American workers who keep it going.

The American people are carrying the heaviest peacetime
tax burden in our nation's history—and it will grow even heavi-
er, under present law, next January. We are taxing ourselves into
economic exhaustion and stagnation, crushing our ability and incentive to save, invest and produce.

This must stop. We must halt this fiscal self-destruction and
restore sanity to our economic system.

I've long advocated a thirty percent reduction in income tax
rates over a period of three years. This phased tax reduction
would begin with a ten percent "down payment" tax cut in 1981,
which the Republicans in Congress and I have already proposed.

A phased reduction of tax rates would go a long way toward easing the heavy burden on the American people. But we
shouldn't stop there.

Within the context of economic conditions and appropriate
budget priorities during each fiscal year of my presidency, I would
strive to go further. This would include improvement in business
depreciation taxes so we can stimulate investment in order to
get plants and equipment replaced, put more Americans back to
work, and put our nation back on the road to being competitive in
world commerce. We will also work to reduce the cost of government as a percentage of our gross national product.

The first task of national leadership is to set realistic and honest priorities in our policies and our budget, and I pledge that my
administration will do that. When I talk of tax cuts, I am reminded that every major tax cut in this century has strengthened the
economy, generated renewed productivity, and ended up yielding
new revenues for the government by creating new investment,
new jobs, and more commerce among our people.

The present administration has been forced by the Republicans to play follow-the-leader with regard to a tax cut. But in this

election year we must take with the proverbial "grain of salt" any tax cut proposed by those who have already given us the greatest tax increase in our nation's history.

When those in leadership give us tax increases and tell us we must also do with less, have they thought about those who've always had less—especially the minorities? This is like telling them that just as they step on the first rung of the ladder of opportunity, the ladder is being pulled out from under them. That may be the Democratic leadership's message to the minorities, but it won't be our message. Ours, ours will be: We have to move ahead, but we're not going to leave anyone behind.

Thanks to the economic policies of the Democratic Party, millions of Americans find themselves out of work. Millions more have never even had a fair chance to learn new skills, hold a decent job or secure for themselves and their families a share in the prosperity of this nation.

It's time to put America back to work, to make our cities and towns resound with the confident voices of men and women of all races, nationalities and faiths bringing home to their families a paycheck they can cash for honest money. For those without skills, we'll find a way to help them get new skills. For those without job opportunities we'll stimulate new opportunities, particularly in the inner cities where they live.

For those who've abandoned hope, we'll restore hope and we'll welcome them into a great national crusade to make America great again.

When we move from domestic affairs and cast our eyes abroad, we see an equally sorry chapter in the record of the present administration:

- A Soviet combat brigade trains in Cuba, just ninety miles from our shores.

- A Soviet army of invasion occupies Afghanistan, further threatening our vital interests in the Middle East.

- America's defense strength is at its lowest ebb in a generation, while the Soviet Union is vastly outspending us in both
  strategic and conventional arms.

- Our European allies, looking nervously at the growing men-
  ace from the east, turn to us for leadership and fail to find it.

- And incredibly, more than fifty—as you've been told from
  this platform so eloquently already—more than fifty of our
  fellow Americans have been held captive for over eight years,
  eight months by a dictatorial foreign power that holds us up
  to ridicule before the world.

Adversaries large and small test our will and seek to confound
our resolve, but we are given weakness when we need strength;
vacillation when the times demand firmness.

The Carter administration lives in the world of make-believe,
every day drawing up a response to that day's problems, troubles, regardless of what happened yesterday and what will happen
tomorrow.

But you and I live in a real world, where disasters are overtak-
ing our nation without any real response from Washington.

This is make-believe, self-deceit, and, above all, transparent
hypocrisy. For example, Mr. Carter says he supports the volunteer
Army, but he lets military pay and benefits slip so low that many
of our enlisted personnel are actually eligible for food stamps. Re-
enlistment rates drop, and just recently, after he fought all week
against a proposed pay increase for our men and women in the
military, he then helicoptered out to our carrier the U.S.S. Nim-
itz, which was returning from long months of duty in the Indian
Ocean, and told the crew of that ship that he advocated better pay
for them and their comrades. Where does he really stand, now
that he's back on shore?

Well, I'll tell you where I stand. I do not favor a peacetime
draft or registration, but I do favor pay and benefit levels that will

attract and keep highly motivated men and women in our volunteer forces and back them up with an active reserve, trained and ready for instant call in case of emergency.

You know, there may be a sailor at the helm of the ship of state, but the ship has no rudder. Critical decisions are made at times almost in comic fashion, but who can laugh?

Who was not embarrassed when the administration handed a major propaganda victory in the United Nations to the enemies of Israel, our staunch Middle East ally for three decades, and then claimed that the American vote was a "mistake," a "failure of communication" between the president, his secretary of state, and the UN ambassador.

Who does not feel a growing sense of unease as our allies, facing repeated instances of an amateurish and confused administration, reluctantly conclude that America is unwilling or unable to fulfill its obligations as leader of the free world. Who does not feel rising alarm when the question in any discussion of foreign policy is no longer, "Should we do something?" but "Do we have the capacity to do anything?"

The administration which has brought us to this state is seeking your endorsement for four more years of weakness, indecision, mediocrity, and incompetence. No. No. No American should vote until he or she has asked: Is the United States stronger and more respected now than it was three and a half years ago? Is the world safer, a safer place in which to live?

It is the responsibility of the President of the United States, in working for peace, to insure that the safety of our people cannot successfully be threatened by a hostile foreign power. As president, fulfilling that responsibility will be my number-one priority. We're not a warlike people. Quite the opposite: we always seek to live in peace. We resort to force infrequently and with great reluctance—and only after we've determined that it is absolutely necessary. We are awed—and rightly so—by the forces of destruction at loose in the world in this nuclear era.

But neither can we be naive or foolish. Four times in my life-time America has gone to war, bleeding the lives of its young men into the sands of island beachheads, the fields of Europe, and the jungles and rice paddies of Asia. We know only too well that war comes not when the forces of freedom are strong; it is when they are weak that tyrants are tempted.

We simply cannot learn these lessons the hard way again with-out risking our destruction.

Of all the objectives we seek, first and foremost is the estab-lishment of lasting world peace. We must always stand ready to negotiate in good faith, ready to pursue any reasonable avenue that holds forth the promise of lessening tensions and furthering the prospects of peace. But let our friends and those who may wish us ill take note: the United States has an obligation to its cit-izens and to the people of the world never to let those who would destroy freedom dictate the future course of life on this planet. I would regard my election as proof that we have renewed our resolve to preserve world peace and freedom, that this nation will once again be strong enough to do that.

Now, this evening marks the last step, save one, of a campaign that has taken Nancy and me from one end of this great nation to the other, over many months and thousands and thousands of miles. There are those who question the way we choose a presi-dent, who say that our process imposes difficult and exhausting burdens on those who seek the office. I have not found it so.

It is impossible to capture in words the splendor of this vast continent, which God has granted as our portion of His creation. There are no words to express the extraordinary strength and character of this breed of people we call Americans. Everywhere we've met thousands of Democrats, Independents, and Repub-licans from all economic conditions and walks of life, bound together in that community of shared values of family, work, neighborhood, peace, and freedom. They are concerned, yes; they're not frightened. They're disturbed, but not dismayed. They are the kind of men and women Tom Paine had in mind when he wrote, during the darkest days of the American Revolution, "We have it in our power to begin the world over again."

Nearly 150 years after Tom Paine wrote those words, an American president told the generation of the Great Depression that it had a "rendezvous with destiny." I believe this generation of Americans today also has a rendezvous with destiny. Tonight, let us dedicate ourselves to renewing the American compact. I ask you not simply to "trust me," but to trust your values—our values—and to hold me responsible for living up to them. I ask you to trust that American spirit which knows no ethnic, religious, social, political, regional, or economic boundaries—the spirit that burned with zeal in the hearts of millions of immigrants from every corner of the earth who came here in search of freedom.

Some say that spirit no longer exists. But I've seen it—I've felt it—all across the land, in the big cities, the small towns, and in rural America. It's still there, ready to blaze into life if you and I are willing to do what has to be done. We have to do the practical things, the down-to-earth things, such as creating policies that will stimulate our economy, increase productivity, and put America back to work. The time is now to limit federal spending; to insist on a stable monetary reform and to free ourselves from imported oil.

The time is now to resolve that the basis of a firm and principled foreign policy is one that takes the world as it is and seeks to change it by leadership and example, not by harangue, harassment, or wishful thinking.

The time is now to say that we shall seek new friendships and expand others and improve others, but we shall not do so by breaking our word or casting aside old friends and allies.

And the time is now to redeem promises once made to the American people by another candidate, in another time and another place. He said:

"For three long years I have been going up and down this country preaching that government—federal, state and local—costs too much. I shall not stop that preaching. As an immediate program of action, we must abolish useless offices. We must eliminate unnecessary functions of government.

"We must consolidate subdivisions of government and, like the private citizen, give up luxuries which we can no longer afford."

And then he said:

"I propose to you, my friends, and through you, that government of all kinds, big and little, be made solvent and that the example be set by the president of the United States and his Cabinet."

That was Franklin Delano Roosevelt's words as he accepted the Democratic nomination for president in 1932.

The time is now, my fellow Americans, to recapture our destiny, to take it into our own hands. And to do this, it will take many of us, working together. I ask you tonight, all over this land, to volunteer your help in this cause so that we can carry our message throughout the land.

Isn't it time that "We the People" carry out these unkept promises? That we pledge to each other and to all America on this July day forty-eight years later, that now we intend to do just that.

I have thought of something that's not a part of my speech and worried over whether I should do it. Can we doubt that only a Divine Providence placed this land, this island of freedom, here as a refuge for all those people in the world who yearn to breathe free? Jews and Christians enduring persecution behind the Iron Curtain; the boat people of Southeast Asia, Cuba, and of Haiti; the victims of drought and famine in Africa; the freedom fighters of Afghanistan; and our own countrymen held in savage captivity.

I'll confess that I've been a little afraid to suggest what I'm going to suggest. I'm more afraid not to. Can we begin our crusade joined together in a moment of silent prayer?

God bless America.

Thank you.

8

"My Pledge"

Reagan's first term came when the country was in economic turmoil and beleaguered by a waffling foreign policy. Finally, as president, Reagan would be able to affect change within a government that, especially under Carter's liberal regime, had grown beyond the will of the people.

Looking back at that era, Reagan recounted, "The year 1981 was one of applying the conservative principles that I had so long espoused to national government. The great exercise was almost cut short by Mr. Hinckley's bullet, which got within an inch of my heart. That slowed me down for a couple of months, but in a way it allowed the pressure for change to build, so that when I was back in the fray I had momentum on my side. I had an agenda. I had things that I wanted to accomplish. I began outlining all that with my inaugural address."

First Inaugural Address

JANUARY 20, 1981

Senator Hatfield, Mr. Chief Justice, Mr. President, Vice President Bush, Vice President Mondale, Senator Baker, Speaker O'Neill, Reverend Moomaw, and my fellow citizens:

To a few of us here today, this is a solemn and most momentous occasion; and yet, in the history of our nation, it is a commonplace occurrence. The orderly transfer of authority as called for in the Constitution routinely takes place as it has for almost two centuries and few of us stop to think how unique we really are. In the eyes of many in the world, this every-four-year ceremony we accept as normal is nothing less than a miracle.

Mr. President, I want our fellow citizens to know how much you did to carry on this tradition. By your gracious cooperation in the transition process, you have shown a watching world that we are a united people pledged to maintaining a political system which guarantees individual liberty to a greater degree than any other, and I thank you and your people for all your help in maintaining the continuity which is the bulwark of our republic.

The business of our nation goes forward. These United States are confronted with an economic affliction of great proportions. We suffer from the longest and one of the worst sustained inflations in our national history. It distorts our economic decisions, penalizes thrift, and crushes the struggling young and the fixed-income elderly alike. It threatens to shatter the lives of millions of our people.

Idle industries have cast workers into unemployment, causing human misery and personal indignity. Those who do work are denied a fair return for their labor by a tax system which penalizes successful achievement and keeps us from maintaining full productivity.

But great as our tax burden is, it has not kept pace with public spending. For decades, we have piled deficit upon deficit, mortgaging our future and our children's future for the temporary convenience of the present. To continue this long trend is to guarantee tremendous social, cultural, political, and economic upheavals.

You and I as individuals can, by borrowing, live beyond our means—but for only a limited period of time. Why, then, should we think that collectively, as a nation, we are not bound by that same limitation?

We must act today in order to preserve tomorrow. And let there be no misunderstanding: we are going to begin to act, beginning today.

The economic ills we suffer have come upon us over several decades. They will not go away in days, weeks, or months, but they will go away. They will go away because we, as Americans, have the capacity now, as we have had in the past, to do whatever needs to be done to preserve this last and greatest bastion of freedom.

In this present crisis, government is not the solution to our problem.

From time to time, we have been tempted to believe that society has become too complex to be managed by self-rule, that government by an elite group is superior to government for, by, and of the people. But if no one among us is capable of governing himself, then who among us has the capacity to govern someone else? All of us together, in and out of government, must bear the burden. The solutions we seek must be equitable, with no one group singled out to pay a higher price.

We hear much of special interest groups. Our concern must be for a special interest group that has been too long neglected. It knows no sectional boundaries or ethnic and racial divisions, and it crosses political party lines. It is made up of men and women who raise our food, patrol our streets, man our mines and our factories, teach our children, keep our homes, and heal us when we are sick—professionals, industrialists, shopkeepers, clerks, cabbies, and truck drivers. They are, in short, "We the People," this breed called Americans.

Well, this administration's objective will be a healthy, vigorous, growing economy that provides equal opportunity for all Americans, with no barriers born of bigotry or discrimination. Putting America back to work means putting all Americans back to work. Ending inflation means freeing all Americans from the terror of runaway living costs. All must share in the productive work of this "new beginning" and all must share in the bounty of a revived economy. With the idealism and fair play which are the core of our system and our strength, we can have a strong and prosperous America at peace with itself and the world.

So, as we begin, let us take inventory. We are a nation that has a government—not the other way around. And this makes us special among the nations of the earth. Our government has no power except that granted it by the people. It is time to check and reverse the growth of government, which shows signs of having grown beyond the consent of the governed.

It is my intention to curb the size and influence of the federal establishment and to demand recognition of the distinction between the powers granted to the federal government and those reserved to the states or to the people. All of us need to be reminded that the federal government did not create the states; the states created the federal government.

Now, so there will be no misunderstanding, it is not my intention to do away with government. It is, rather, to make it work—work with us, not over us; to stand by our side, not ride on our back. Government can and must provide opportunity, not smother it; foster productivity, not stifle it.

If we look to the answer as to why, for so many years, we achieved so much, prospered as no other people on earth, it was because here, in this land, we unleashed the energy and individual genius of man to a greater extent than has ever been done before. Freedom and the dignity of the individual have been more available and assured here than in any other place on earth. The price for this freedom at times has been high, but we have never been unwilling to pay that price.

It is no coincidence that our present troubles parallel and are proportionate to the intervention and intrusion in our lives that result from unnecessary and excessive growth of government. It is time for us to realize that we are too great a nation to limit ourselves to small dreams. We are not, as some would have us believe, doomed to an inevitable decline. I do not believe in a fate that will fall on us no matter what we do. I do believe in a fate that will fall on us if we do nothing.

So, with all the creative energy at our command, let us begin an era of national renewal. Let us renew our determination, our courage, and our strength. And let us renew our faith and our hope.

We have every right to dream heroic dreams. Those who say that we are in a time when there are no heroes just don't know where to look. You can see heroes every day going in and out of factory gates. Others, a handful in number, produce enough food to feed all of us and then the world beyond. You meet heroes across a counter—and they are on both sides of that counter. There are entrepreneurs with faith in themselves and faith in an idea who create new jobs, new wealth, and opportunity. They are individuals and families whose taxes support the government and whose voluntary gifts support church, charity, culture, art, and education. Their patriotism is quiet but deep. Their values sustain our national life.

I have used the words "they" and "their" in speaking of these heroes. I could say "you" and "your" because I am addressing the heroes of whom I speak—you, the citizens of this blessed land. Your dreams, your hopes, your goals are going to be the dreams, the hopes, and the goals of this administration, so help me God.

We shall reflect the compassion that is so much a part of your makeup. How can we love our country and not love our countrymen—and, loving them, reach out a hand when they fall, heal them when they are sick, and provide opportunities to make them self-sufficient so they will be equal in fact and not just in theory?

Can we solve the problems confronting us? Well, the answer is an unequivocal and emphatic "Yes!" To paraphrase Winston Churchill, I did not take the oath I have just taken with the intention of presiding over the dissolution of the world's strongest economy.

In the days ahead I will propose removing the roadblocks that have slowed our economy and reduced productivity. Steps will be taken aimed at restoring the balance between the various levels of government. Progress may be slow—measured in inches and feet, not miles—but we will progress. It is time to reawaken this industrial giant, to get government back within its means, and to lighten our punitive tax burden. And these will be our first priorities, and on these principles there will be no compromise.

On the eve of our struggle for independence, a man who might have been one of the greatest among the Founding Fathers, Dr. Joseph Warren, president of the Massachusetts Congress, said to his fellow Americans: "Our country is in danger, but not to be despaired of. On you depend the fortunes of America. You are to decide the important questions upon which rests the happiness and the liberty of millions yet unborn. Act worthy of yourselves."

Well, I believe we, the Americans of today, are ready to act worthy of ourselves, ready to do what must be done to ensure happiness and liberty for ourselves, our children, and our children's children.

And as we renew ourselves here in our own land, we will be seen as having greater strength throughout the world. We will again be the exemplar of freedom and a beacon of hope for those who do not now have freedom.

To those neighbors and allies who share our freedom, we will strengthen our historic ties and assure them of our support and firm commitment. We will match loyalty with loyalty. We will strive for mutually beneficial relations. We will not use our friendship to impose on their sovereignty, for our own sovereignty is not for sale.

As for the enemies of freedom, those who are potential adversaries, they will be reminded that peace is the highest aspiration of the American people. We will negotiate for it, sacrifice for it; we will not surrender for it—now or ever.

Our forbearance should never be misunderstood. Our reluctance for conflict should not be misjudged as a failure of will. When action is required to preserve our national security, we will act. We will maintain sufficient strength to prevail if need be, knowing that if we do so we have the best chance of never having to use that strength.

Above all, we must realize that no arsenal, or no weapon in the arsenals of the world, is so formidable as the will and moral courage of free men and women. It is a weapon our adversaries in today's world do not have. It is a weapon that we as Americans do have. Let that be understood by those who practice terrorism and prey upon their neighbors.

I am told that tens of thousands of prayer meetings are being held on this day, and for that I am deeply grateful. We are a nation under God, and I believe God intended for us to be free. It would be fitting and good, I think, if on each Inauguration Day in future years it should be declared a day of prayer.

This is the first time in history that this ceremony has been held, as you have been told, on this West Front of the Capitol. Standing here, one faces a magnificent vista, opening up on this city's special beauty and history. At the end of this open mall are those shrines to the giants on whose shoulders we stand.

Directly in front of me, the monument to a monumental man: George Washington, father of our country. A man of humility who came to greatness reluctantly. He led America out of revolutionary victory into infant nationhood. Off to one side, the stately memorial to Thomas Jefferson. The Declaration of Independence flames with his eloquence.

And then beyond the Reflecting Pool, the dignified columns of the Lincoln Memorial. Whoever would understand in his heart the meaning of America will find it in the life of Abraham Lincoln.

Beyond those monuments to heroism is the Potomac River, and on the far shore the sloping hills of Arlington National Cemetery with its row on row of simple white markers bearing crosses or Stars of David. They add up to only a tiny fraction of the price that has been paid for our freedom.

Each one of those markers is a monument to the kinds of hero I spoke of earlier. Their lives ended in places called Belleau Wood, The Argonne, Omaha Beach, Salerno, and halfway around the world on Guadalcanal, Tarawa, Pork Chop Hill, the Chosin Reservoir, and in a hundred rice paddies and jungles of a place called Vietnam.

Under one such marker lies a young man, Martin Treptow, who left his job in a small-town barber shop in 1917 to go to France with the famed Rainbow Division. There, on the western front, he was killed trying to carry a message between battalions under heavy artillery fire.

We are told that on his body was found a diary. On the flyleaf, under the heading "My Pledge," he had written these words: "America must win this war. Therefore, I will work, I will save, I will sacrifice, I will endure, I will fight cheerfully and do my utmost, as if the issue of the whole struggle depended on me alone."

The crisis we are facing today does not require of us the kind of sacrifice that Martin Treptow and so many thousands of others were called upon to make. It does require, however, our best effort, and our willingness to believe in ourselves and to believe in our capacity to perform great deeds; to believe that together, with God's help, we can and will resolve the problems which now confront us.

And, after all, why shouldn't we believe that? We are Americans. God bless you, and thank you.

9

ECONOMIC
RECOVERY PROGRAM

Just shy of a month after being wounded in an assassination attempt by John Hinckley, Jr., a psychotic loner, Reagan was given a hero's welcome before addressing a joint session of Congress and greeted with a momentous standing ovation. Though ever gracious, Reagan was quick to start his address to focus on the task at hand: rebuilding our damaged economy.

As Reagan presented his recovery package before Congress, even the most liberal of audience members were pleased to find bipartisan incentives that readily extended the bill across the aisle. Reagan understood how to implement practicality measures, such as minimizing welfare programs and stifling inflation while creating job opportunities. He knew how to reduce taxes to encourage personal investment, stimulate business, and create more jobs. Along with cuts in government spending, these steps would lead to a balanced budget.

Making history, the Great Communicator would forever be synonymous with the budgetary balancing method that he created: Reaganomics.

Address to a Joint Session of Congress

APRIL 28, 1981
FIRST SPEECH AFTER ASSASSINATION ATTEMPT

———

You wouldn't want to talk me into an encore, would you? [Applause and laugter] Mr. Speaker, Mr. President, distinguished members of the Congress, honored guests, and fellow citizens:

I have no words to express my appreciation for that greeting. I have come to speak to you tonight about our economic recovery program and why I believe it's essential that the Congress approve this package, which I believe will lift the crushing burden of inflation off of our citizens and restore the vitality to our economy and our industrial machine.

First, however, and due to events of the past few weeks, will you permit me to digress for a moment from the all-important subject of why we must bring government spending under control and reduce tax rates. I'd like to say a few words directly to all of you and to those who are watching and listening tonight, because this is the only way I know to express to all of you, on behalf of Nancy and myself, our appreciation for your messages and flowers and, most of all, your prayers, not only for me but for those others who fell beside me. The warmth of your words, the expression of friendship and, yes, love, meant more to us than you can ever know. You have given us a memory that we'll treasure forever. And you've provided an answer to those few voices that were raised saying that what happened was evidence that ours is a sick society.

The society we heard from is made up of millions of compassionate Americans and their children, from college age to kindergarten. As a matter of fact, as evidence of that I have a letter with me. The letter came from Peter Sweeney. He's in the second grade in the Riverside School in Rockville Centre, and he said, "I hope you get well quick or you might have to make a speech in your pajamas." [Laughter] And he added a postscript: "P.S. If you have to make a speech in your pajamas, I warned you." [Laughter]

Well, sick societies don't produce men like the two who recently returned from outer space. Sick societies don't produce young men like Secret Service agent Tim McCarthy, who placed his body—he placed his body between mine and the man with the gun simply because he felt that's what his duty called for him to do. Sick societies don't produce dedicated police officers like Tom Delahanty or able and devoted public servants like Jim Brady. Sick societies don't make people like us so proud to be Americans and so very proud of our fellow citizens.

Now, let's talk about getting spending and inflation under control and cutting your tax rates. Mr. Speaker and Senator Baker, I want to thank you for your cooperation in helping to arrange this joint session of the Congress. I won't be speaking to you very long tonight, but I asked for this meeting because the urgency of our joint mission has not changed. Thanks to some very fine people, my health is much improved. I'd like to be able to say that with regard to the health of the economy.

It's been half a year since the election that charged all of us in this government with the task of restoring our economy. And where have we come in this six months? Inflation, as measured by the Consumer Price Index, has continued at a double-digit rate. Mortgage interest rates have averaged almost fifteen percent for these six months, preventing families across America from buying homes. There are still almost 8 million unemployed. The average worker's hourly earnings after adjusting for inflation are lower today than they were six months ago, and there have been over 6,000 business failures.

Six months is long enough. The American people now want us to act, and not in half-measures. They demand and they've earned a full and comprehensive effort to clean up our economic mess. Because of the extent of our economy's sickness, we know that the cure will not come quickly and that even with our package, progress will come in inches and feet, not in miles. But to fail to act will delay even longer and more painfully the cure which must come. And that cure begins with the federal budget. And the budgetary actions taken by the Congress over the next few days will determine how we respond to the message of last November 4. That message was very simple: Our government is too big, and it spends too much.

For the last few months, you and I have enjoyed a relationship based on extraordinary cooperation. Because of this cooperation we've come a long distance in less than three months. I want to thank the leadership of the Congress for helping in setting a fair timetable for consideration of our recommendations. And committee chairmen on both sides of the aisle have called prompt and thorough hearings. We have also communicated in a spirit of candor, openness and mutual respect. Tonight, as our decision day nears and as the House of Representatives weighs its alternatives, I wish to address you in that same spirit.

The Senate Budget Committee, under the leadership of Pete Domenici, has just today voted out a budget resolution supported by Democrats and Republicans alike that is in all major respects consistent with the program that we have proposed. Now we look forward to favorable action on the Senate floor, but an equally crucial test involves the House of Representatives. The House will soon be choosing between two different versions or measures to deal with the economy. One is the measure offered by the House Budget Committee. The other is a bipartisan measure, a substitute introduced by Congressmen Phil Gramm of Texas and Del Latta of Ohio.

On behalf of the administration, let me say that we embrace and fully support that bipartisan substitute. It will achieve all the essential aims of controlling government spending, reducing the tax burden, building a national defense second to none, stimulating economic growth, and creating millions of new jobs. At the same time, however, I must state our opposition to the measure offered by the House Budget Committee. It may appear that we have two alternatives. In reality, however, there are no more alternatives left.

The committee measure quite simply falls far too short of the essential actions that we must take. For example, in the next three years, the committee measure projects spending $141 billion more than does the bipartisan substitute. It regrettably cuts over $14 billion in essential defense spending, funding required to restore America's national security. It adheres to the failed policy of trying to balance the budget on the taxpayer's back. It would increase tax payments over a third, adding up to a staggering quarter of a trillion dollars. Federal taxes would increase twelve percent each year. Taxpayers would be paying a larger share of their income to the government in 1984 than they do at present. In short, that measure reflects an echo of the past rather than a benchmark for the future. High taxes and excess spending growth created our present economic mess; more of the same will not cure the hardship, anxiety, and discouragement it has imposed on the American people.

Let us cut through the fog for a moment. The answer to a government that's too big is to stop feeding its growth. Government spending has been growing faster than the economy itself. The massive national debt which we accumulated is the result of the government's high spending diet. Well, it's time to change the diet and to change it in the right way.

I know the tax portion of our package is of concern to some of you. Let me make a few points that I feel have been overlooked. First of all, it should be looked at as an integral part of the entire package, not something separate and apart from the budget reductions, the regulatory relief, and the monetary restraints. Probably the most common misconception is that we are proposing to reduce government revenues to less than what the government has been receiving. This is not true. Actually, the discussion has to do with how much of a tax increase should be imposed on the taxpayer in 1982.

Now, I know that over the recess in some informal polling some of your constituents have been asked which they'd rather have, a balanced budget or a tax cut, and with the common sense that characterizes the people of this country, the answer, of course, has been a balanced budget. But may I suggest, with no inference that there was wrong intent on the part of those who asked the question, the question was inappropriate to the situation. Our choice is not between a balanced budget and a tax cut. Properly asked, the question is, "Do you want a great big raise in your taxes this coming year or, at the worst, a very little increase with the prospect of tax reduction and a balanced budget down the road a ways?" With the common sense that the people have already shown, I'm sure we all know what the answer to that question would be.

A gigantic tax increase has been built into the system. We propose nothing more than a reduction of that increase. The people have a right to know that even with our plan they will be paying more in taxes, but not as much more as they will without it. The option, I believe, offered by the House Budget Committee, will leave spending too high and tax rates too high. At the same time, I think it cuts the defense budget too much, and by attempting to reduce the deficit through higher taxes, it will not create the kind of strong economic growth and the new jobs that we must have.

Let us not overlook the fact that the small, independent business man or woman creates more than eighty percent of all the new jobs and employs more than half of our total work force. Our across-the-board cut in tax rates for a three-year period will give them much of the incentive and promise of stability they need to go forward with expansion plans calling for additional employees.

Tonight I renew my call for us to work as a team, to join in cooperation so that we find answers which will begin to solve all our economic problems and not just some of them. The economic recovery package that I've outlined to you over the past weeks is, I deeply believe, the only answer that we have left. Reducing the growth of spending, cutting marginal tax rates, providing relief from overregulation, and following a noninflationary and predictable monetary policy are interwoven measures which will ensure that we have addressed each of the severe dislocations which threaten our economic future. These policies will make our economy stronger; and the stronger economy will balance the budget, which we're committed to do by 1984.

When I took the oath of office, I pledged loyalty to only one special interest group: "We the People." Those people—neighbors and friends, shopkeepers and laborers, farmers and craftsmen— do not have infinite patience. As a matter of fact, some eighty years ago Teddy Roosevelt wrote these instructive words in his first message to the Congress: "The American people are slow to wrath, but when their wrath is once kindled, it burns like a consuming flame." Well, perhaps that kind of wrath will be deserved if our answer to these serious problems is to repeat the mistakes of the past.

The old and comfortable way is to shave a little here and a little there. Well, that's not acceptable anymore. I think this great and historic Congress knows that way is no longer acceptable. [Applause] Thank you very much. Thank you. I think you've shown that you know the one sure way to continue the inflationary spiral is to fall back into the predictable patterns of old economic practices. Isn't it time that we tried something new? When you allowed me to speak to you here in these chambers a little earlier, I told you that I wanted this program for economic recovery to be ours—yours and mine. I think the bipartisan substitute bill has achieved that purpose. It moves us toward economic vitality.

Just two weeks ago, you and I joined millions of our fellow Americans in marveling at the magic historical moment that John Young and Bob Crippen created in their space shuttle Columbia. The last manned effort was almost six years ago, and, I remembered, on this more recent day, over the years how we'd all come to expect technological precision of our men and machines. And each amazing achievement became commonplace, until the next new challenge was raised. With the space shuttle we tested our ingenuity once again, moving beyond the accomplishments of the past into the promise and uncertainty of the future. Thus, we not only planned to send up a 122-foot aircraft 170 miles into space, but we also intended to make it maneuverable and return it to earth, landing ninety-eight tons of exotic metals delicately on a remote dry lake bed. The space shuttle did more than prove our technological abilities. It raised our expectations once more. It started us dreaming again.

The poet Carl Sandburg wrote: "The republic is a dream. Nothing happens unless first a dream." And that's what makes us, as Americans, different. We've always reached for a new spirit and aimed at a higher goal. We've been courageous and determined, unafraid and bold. Who among us wants to be first to say we no longer have those qualities, that we must limp along, doing the same things that have brought us our present misery?

I believe that the people you and I represent are ready to chart a new course. They look to us to meet the great challenge, to reach beyond the commonplace and not fall short for lack of creativity or courage. Someone you know has said that he who would have nothing to do with thorns must never attempt to gather flowers. Well, we have much greatness before us. We can restore our economic strength and build opportunities like none we've ever had before. As Carl Sandburg said, all we need to begin with is a dream that we can do better than before. All we need to have is faith, and that dream will come true. All we need to do is act, and the time for action is now. Thank you. Good night.

10

THE CRUSADE FOR FREEDOM

Recognized as Ronald Reagan's first in a series of speeches in which he would publicly solidify his Soviet "evil empire" stance, the "Westminster Address" marked the first time a U.S. president spoke out against the communist system of government. The actual phrase, "evil empire," wouldn't be used until 1983, when his vehement opposition to the ideology would reach its peak.

Countless historians agree that Reagan predicted the demise of communism. He used Leon Trotsky's phrase, declaring that Marxism and Leninism will end up "on the ash heap of history."

Mikhail Gorbachev's arrival onto the political scene represented a sense of hope for Reagan and his cause. In Gorbachev, he would find a Soviet leader with whom he could actually communicate. Together, they would work to end the arms race and retire communism in the Soviet Union, making the world a safer place while advancing the cause of freedom.

Address to the British Parliament, House of Commons, London

JUNE 8, 1982

———

W e're approaching the end of a bloody century plagued by a terrible political invention—totalitarianism. Optimism comes less easily today, not because democracy is less vigorous but because democracy's enemies have refined their instruments of repression. Yet optimism is in order, because, day by day, democracy is proving itself to be a not at all fragile flower. From Stettin on the Baltic to Varna on the Black Sea, the regimes planted by totalitarianism have had more than thirty years to establish their legitimacy. But none—not one regime—has yet been able to risk free elections. Regimes planted by bayonets do not take root.

The strength of the Solidarity movement in Poland demonstrates the truth told in an underground joke in the Soviet Union. It is that the Soviet Union would remain a one-party nation even if an opposition party were permitted, because everyone would join the opposition party.

Historians looking back at our time will note the consistent restraint and peaceful intentions of the West. They will note that it was the democracies who refused to use the threat of their nuclear monopoly in the forties and early fifties for territorial or imperial gain. Had that nuclear monopoly been in the hands of the Communist world, the map of Europe—indeed, the world—would look very different today. And certainly they will note it was not the democracies that invaded Afghanistan or suppressed Polish Solidarity or used chemical and toxin warfare in Afghanistan and Southeast Asia.

If history teaches anything, it teaches self-delusion in the face of unpleasant facts is folly. We see around us today the marks of our terrible dilemma: predictions of doomsday, antinuclear demonstrations, an arms race in which the West must, for its own protection, be an unwilling participant. At the same time we see totalitarian forces in the world who seek subversion and conflict around the globe to further their barbarous assault on the human spirit. What, then, is our course? Must civilization perish in a hail of fiery atoms? Must freedom wither in a quiet, deadening accommodation with totalitarian evil?

Sir Winston Churchill refused to accept the inevitability of war or even that it was imminent. He said, "I do not believe that Soviet Russia desires war. What they desire is the fruits of war and the indefinite expansion of their power and doctrines. But what we have to consider here today while time remains is the permanent prevention of war and the establishment of conditions of freedom and democracy as rapidly as possible in all countries."

Well, this is precisely our mission today: to preserve freedom as well as peace. It may not be easy to see, but I believe we live now at a turning point.

In an ironic sense Karl Marx was right. We are witnessing today a great revolutionary crisis, a crisis where the demands of the economic order are conflicting directly with those of the political order. But the crisis is happening not in the free, non-Marxist West but in the home of Marxism-Leninism, the Soviet Union. It is the Soviet Union that runs against the tide of history by denying human freedom and human dignity to its citizens. It also is in deep economic difficulty. The rate of growth in the national product has been steadily declining since the fifties and is less than half of what it was then.

The dimensions of this failure are astounding: a country which employs one-fifth of its population in agriculture is unable to feed its own people. Were it not for the private sector, the tiny private sector tolerated in Soviet agriculture, the country might be on the brink of famine. These private plots occupy a bare three percent of the arable land but account for nearly one-quarter of

Soviet farm output and nearly one-third of meat products and vegetables. Over-centralized, with little or no incentives, year after year the Soviet system pours its best resources into the making of instruments of destruction. The constant shrinkage of economic growth combined with the growth of military production is putting a heavy strain on the Soviet people. What we see here is a political structure that no longer corresponds to its economic base, a society where productive forces are hampered by political ones.

The decay of the Soviet experiment should come as no surprise to us. Wherever the comparisons have been made between free and closed societies—West Germany and East Germany, Austria and Czechoslovakia, Malaysia and Vietnam—it is the democratic countries that are prosperous and responsive to the needs of their people. And one of the simple but overwhelming facts of our time is this: of all the millions of refugees we've seen in the modern world, their flight is always away from, not toward, the Communist world. Today on the NATO line, our military forces face east to prevent a possible invasion. On the other side of the line, the Soviet forces also face east—to prevent their people from leaving.

The hard evidence of totalitarian rule has caused in mankind an uprising of the intellect and will. Whether it is the growth of the new schools of economics in America or England, or the appearance of the so-called new philosophers in France, there is one unifying thread running through the intellectual work of these groups—rejection of the arbitrary power of the state, the refusal to subordinate the rights of the individual to the superstate, the realization that collectivism stifles all the best human impulses.

Chairman Brezhnev repeatedly has stressed that the competition of ideas and systems must continue and that this is entirely consistent with relaxation of tensions and peace.

Well, we ask only that these systems begin by living up to their own constitutions, abiding by their own laws, and complying with the international obligations they have undertaken. We ask only for a process, a direction, a basic code of decency, not for an instant transformation.

We cannot ignore the fact that even without our encouragement, there has been and will continue to be repeated explosions against repression and dictatorships. The Soviet Union itself is not immune to this reality. Any system is inherently unstable that has no peaceful means to legitimize its leaders. In such cases, the very repressiveness of the state ultimately drives people to resist it, if necessary, by force.

While we must be cautious about forcing the pace of change, we must not hesitate to declare our ultimate objectives and to take concrete actions to move toward them. We must be staunch in our conviction that freedom is not the sole prerogative of a lucky few, but the inalienable and universal right of all human beings. So states the United Nations Universal Declaration of Human Rights, which, among other things, guarantees free elections.

The objective I propose is quite simple to state: to foster the infrastructure of democracy—the system of a free press, unions, political parties, universities—which allows a people to choose their own way to develop their own culture, to reconcile their own differences through peaceful means.

This is not cultural imperialism; it is providing the means for genuine self-determination and protection for diversity. Democracy already flourishes in countries with very different cultures and historical experiences. It would be cultural condescension, or worse, to say that any people prefer dictatorship to democracy. Who would voluntarily choose not to have the right to vote, decide to purchase government propaganda handouts instead of independent newspapers, prefer government to worker-controlled unions, opt for land to be owned by the state instead of those who till it, want government repression of religious liberty, a single political party instead of a free choice, a rigid cultural orthodoxy instead of democratic tolerance and diversity.

Since 1917, the Soviet Union has given covert political training and assistance to Marxist-Leninists in many countries. Of course, it also has promoted the use of violence and subversion by these same forces. Over the past several decades, West European and other social democrats, Christian democrats, and leaders have offered open assistance to fraternal, political, and social institutions to bring about peaceful and democratic progress. Appropriately, for a vigorous new democracy, the Federal Republic of Germany's political foundations have become a major force in this effort.

We in America now intend to take additional steps, as many of our allies have already done, toward realizing this same goal. The chairmen and other leaders of the national Republican and Democratic Party organizations are initiating a study with the bipartisan American Political Foundation to determine how the United States can best contribute as a nation to the global campaign for democracy now gathering force. They will have the cooperation of congressional leaders of both parties, along with representatives of business, labor, and other major institutions in our society. I look forward to receiving their recommendations and to working with these institutions and the Congress in the common task of strengthening democracy throughout the world.

It is time that we committed ourselves as a nation—in both the public and private sectors—to assisting democratic development.

What I am describing now is a plan and a hope for the long term—the march of freedom and democracy which will leave Marxism-Leninism on the ash heap of history, as it has left other tyrannies which stifle the freedom and muzzle the self-expression of the people. And that's why we must continue our efforts to strengthen NATO even as we move forward with our zero-option initiative in the negotiations on intermediate-range forces and our proposal for a one-third reduction in strategic ballistic missile warheads.

Our military strength is a prerequisite to peace, but let it be clear we maintain this strength in the hope it will never be used, for the ultimate determinant in the struggle that is now going on in the world will not be bombs and rockets but a test of wills and ideas, a trial of spiritual resolve, the values we hold, the beliefs we cherish, the ideals to which we are dedicated.

The British people know that, given strong leadership, time and a little bit of hope, the forces of good ultimately rally and triumph over evil. Here among you is the cradle of self-government, the mother of Parliaments. Here is the enduring greatness of the British contribution to mankind, the great civilized ideas: individual liberty, representative government, and the rule of law under God.

I've often wondered about the shyness of some of us in the West about standing for these ideals that have done so much to ease the plight of man and the hardships of our imperfect world. This reluctance to use those vast resources at our command reminds me of the elderly lady whose home was bombed in the blitz. As the rescuers moved about, they found a bottle of brandy she'd stored behind the staircase, which was all that was left standing. And since she was barely conscious, one of the workers pulled the cork to give her a taste of it. She came around immediately and said, "There, now—put it back. That's for emergencies."

Well, the emergency is upon us. Let us be shy no longer. Let us go to our strength. Let us offer hope. Let us tell the world that a new age is not only possible but probable.

During the dark days of the Second World War, when this island was incandescent with courage, Winston Churchill exclaimed about Britain's adversaries, "What kind of people do they think we are?" Well, Britain's adversaries found out what extraordinary people the British are. But all the democracies paid a terrible price for allowing the dictators to underestimate us. We dare not make that mistake again. So let us ask ourselves, "What kind of people do we think we are?" And let us answer, "Free people, worthy of freedom and determined not only to remain so but to help others gain their freedom as well."

Sir Winston led his people to great victory in war and then lost an election just as the fruits of victory were about to be enjoyed. But he left office honorably and, as it turned out, temporarily, knowing that the liberty of his people was more important than the fate of any single leader. History recalls his greatness in ways no dictator will ever know. And he left us a message of hope for the future, as timely now as when he first uttered it, as opposition leader in the Commons nearly twenty-seven years ago, when he said, "When we look back on all the perils through which we have passed and at the mighty foes that we have laid low and all the dark and deadly designs that we have frustrated, why should we fear for our future? We have," he said, "come safely through the worst."

Well, the task I've set forth will long outlive our own generation. But together we, too, have come through the worst. Let us now begin a major effort to secure the best—a crusade for freedom that will engage the faith and fortitude of the next generation. For the sake of peace and justice, let us move toward a world in which all people are at last free to determine their own destiny.

11

AGENDA FOR PEACE

Again continuing to express his concern for the growing development of nuclear arms by the Soviet Union, here Reagan stressed the choice of the United States to not develop or use further nuclear weapons but instead compromise with other nations to cancel development of some ballistic and cruise missiles. Reagan urged the Soviet Union and other members of the Warsaw Pact to reach an agreement, after nearly a decade of talks, as well as to implement the 1975 Helsinki agreement on security and cooperation in Europe. Not unlike concerns today about Iraq's nuclear plants, Reagan called for independent verification to insure that chemical weapons in Laos and Afghanistan were no longer being used. In spite of the ongoing concerns with the Soviet Union, the President specifically called for ways to increase communication with the Soviets during times of both peace and crisis.

Address to the General Assembly of the United Nations, New York City

JUNE 17, 1982

Mr. Secretary-General, Mr. President, distinguished delegates, ladies and gentlemen:

I speak today as a citizen both of the United States and of the world. I come with the heartfelt wishes of my people for peace, bearing honest proposals and looking for genuine progress.

Dag Hammarskjold said twenty-four years ago this month, "We meet in a time of peace, which is no peace." His words are as true today as they were then. More than a hundred disputes have disturbed the peace among nations since World War II, and today the threat of nuclear disaster hangs over the lives of all our people. The Bible tells us there will be a time for peace, but so far this century mankind has failed to find it.

The United Nations is dedicated to world peace, and its Charter clearly prohibits the international use of force. Yet the tide of belligerence continues to rise. The Charter's influence has weakened even in the four years since the first special session on disarmament. We must not only condemn aggression, we must enforce the dictates of our Charter and resume the struggle for peace.

The record of history is clear: citizens of the United States resort to force reluctantly and only when they must. Our foreign policy, as President Eisenhower once said, "is not difficult to state. We are for peace first, last, and always, for very simple reasons." We know that only in a peaceful atmosphere, a peace with justice, one in which we can be confident, can America prosper as we have known prosperity in the past, he said.

He said to those who challenge the truth of those words, let me point out at the end of World War II, we were the only undamaged industrial power in the world. Our military supremacy was unquestioned. We had harnessed the atom and had the ability to unleash its destructive force anywhere in the world. In short, we could have achieved world domination, but that was contrary to the character of our people. Instead, we have made specific, reasonable, and equitable proposals.

In February, our negotiating team in Geneva offered the Soviet Union a draft treaty on intermediate-range nuclear forces. We offered to cancel deployment of our Pershing II ballistic missiles and ground-launched cruise missiles in exchange for Soviet elimination of the SS-20, SS-4, and SS-5 missiles. This proposal would eliminate with one stroke those systems about which both sides have expressed the greatest concern.

The United States is also looking forward to beginning negotiations on strategic arms reductions with the Soviet Union in less than two weeks. We will work hard to make these talks an opportunity for real progress in our quest for peace.

On May 9th, I announced a phased approach to the reduction of strategic arms. In a first phase, the number of ballistic missile warheads on each side would be reduced to about 5,000. No more than half the remaining warheads would be on land-based missiles. All ballistic missiles would be reduced to an equal level, at about one-half the current United States number. In the second phase, we would reduce each side's overall destructive power to equal levels, including a mutual ceiling on ballistic missile throw-weight below the current U.S. level. We are also prepared to discuss other elements of the strategic balance.

Before I returned from Europe last week, I met in Bonn with the leaders of the North Atlantic Treaty Organization. We agreed to introduce a major new Western initiative for the Vienna negotiations on Mutual Balanced Force Reductions. Our approach calls for common, collective ceilings for both NATO and the Warsaw

Treaty Organization. After seven years, there would be a total of 700,000 ground forces and 900,000 ground and Air Force personnel combined. It also includes a package of associated measures to encourage cooperation and verify compliance.

We urge the Soviet Union and members of the Warsaw Pact to view our Western proposal as a means to reach agreement in Vienna after nine long years of inconclusive talks. We also urge them to implement the 1975 Helsinki agreement on security and cooperation in Europe.

Let me stress that for agreements to work, both sides must be able to verify compliance. The building of mutual confidence in compliance can only be achieved through greater openness. I encourage the special session on disarmament to endorse the importance of these principles in arms control agreements. I have instructed our representatives at the forty-nation Committee on Disarmament to renew emphasis on verification and compliance. Based on a U.S. proposal, a committee has been formed to examine these issues as they relate to restrictions on nuclear testing.

We are also pressing the need for effective verification provisions in agreements banning chemical weapons. The use of chemical and biological weapons has long been viewed with revulsion by civilized nations. No peacemaking institution can ignore the use of those dread weapons and still live up to its mission. The need for a truly effective and verifiable chemical weapons agreement has been highlighted by recent events. The Soviet Union and their allies are violating the Geneva Protocol of 1925, related rules of international law, and the 1972 Biological Weapons Convention. There is conclusive evidence that the Soviet government has provided toxins for use in Laos and Kampuchea, and are themselves using chemical weapons against freedom fighters in Afghanistan.

We have repeatedly protested to the Soviet government, as well as to the governments of Laos and Vietnam, their use of chemical and toxin weapons. We call upon them now to grant full and free access to their countries or to territories they control so that United Nations experts can conduct an effective, independent investigation to verify cessation of these horrors.

Evidence of noncompliance with existing arms control agreements underscores the need to approach negotiation of any new agreements with care. The democracies of the West are open societies. Information on our defenses is available to our citizens, our elected officials, and the world. We do not hesitate to inform potential adversaries of our military forces and ask in return for the same information concerning theirs.

The amount and type of military spending by a country is important for the world to know, as a measure of its intentions and the threat that country may pose to its neighbors. The Soviet Union and other closed societies go to extraordinary lengths to hide their true military spending, not only from other nations but from their own people. This practice contributes to distrust and fear about their intentions.

Today, the United States proposes an international conference on military expenditures to build on the work of this body in developing a common system for accounting and reporting. We urge the Soviet Union, in particular, to join this effort in good faith, to revise the universally discredited official figures it publishes, and to join with us in giving the world a true account of the resources we allocate to our armed forces.

Last Friday in Berlin, I said that I would leave no stone unturned in the effort to reinforce peace and lessen the risk of war. It's been clear to me steps should be taken to improve mutual communication, confidence, and lessen the likelihood of misinterpretation. I have, therefore, directed the exploration of ways to increase understanding and communication between the United States and the Soviet Union in times of peace and of crisis.

We will approach the Soviet Union with proposals for reciprocal exchanges in such areas as advance notification of major strategic exercises that otherwise might be misinterpreted; advance notification of ICBM launches within, as well as beyond, national boundaries; and an expanded exchange of strategic forces data.

While substantial information on U.S. activities and forces in these areas already is provided, I believe that jointly and regularly sharing information would represent a qualitative improvement in the strategic nuclear environment and would help reduce the chance of misunderstandings. I call upon the Soviet Union to join the United States in exploring these possibilities to build confidence, and I ask for your support of our efforts.

Once of the major items before this conference is the development of a comprehensive program of disarmament. We support the effort to chart a course of realistic and effective measures in the quest for peace.

I have come to this hall to call for international recommitment to the basic tenet of the United Nations Charter—that all members practice tolerance and live together in peace as good neighbors under the rule of law, forsaking armed force as a means of settling disputes between nations. America urges you to support the agenda for peace that I have outlined today. We ask you to reinforce the bilateral and multilateral arms control negotiations between members of NATO and the Warsaw Pact, and to rededicate yourselves to maintaining international peace and security and removing threats to peace.

We, who have signed the UN Charter, have pledged to refrain from the threat or use of force against the territory or independence of any state. In these times when more and more lawless acts are going unpunished—as some members of this very body show a growing disregard for the UN Charter—the peace-loving nations of the world must condemn aggression and pledge again to act in a way that is worthy of the ideals that we have endorsed. Let us finally make the Charter live.

In late spring, thirty-seven years ago, representatives of fifty nations gathered on the other side of this continent, in the San Francisco Opera House. The League of Nations had crumbled, and World War II still raged. But those men and nations were determined to find peace. The result was this Charter for peace that is the framework of the United Nations.

President Harry Truman spoke of the revival of an old faith. He said the everlasting moral force of justice prompting that United Nations conference—such a force remains strong in America and in other countries where speech is free and citizens have the right to gather and make their opinions known. And President Truman said, "If we should pay merely lip service to inspiring ideals, and later do violence to simple justice, we would draw down upon us the bitter wrath of generations yet unborn." Those words of Harry Truman have special meaning for us today as we live with the potential to destroy civilization.

"We must learn to live together in peace," he said. "We must build a new world—a far better world." What a better world it would be if the guns were silent, if neighbor no longer encroached on neighbor, and all peoples were free to reap the rewards of their toil and determine their own destiny and system of government, whatever their choice.

During my recent audience with His Holiness, Pope John Paul II, I gave him the pledge of the American people to do everything possible for peace and arms reduction. The American people believe forging real and lasting peace to be their sacred trust. Let us never forget that such a peace would be a terrible hoax if the world were no longer blessed with freedom and respect for human rights.

"The United Nations," Hammarskjold said, "was born out of the cataclysms of war. It should justify the sacrifices of all those who have died for freedom and justice. It is our duty to the past." Hammarskjold said, "And it is our duty to the future to serve both our nations and the world."

As both patriots of our nations and the hope of all the world, let those of us assembled here in the name of peace deepen our understandings, renew our commitment to the rule of law, and take new and bolder steps to calm an uneasy world. Can any delegate here deny that in so doing he would be doing what the people, the rank and file of his own county or her own country want him or her to do? Isn't it time for us to really represent the deepest, most heartfelt yearnings of all of our people?

Let no nation abuse this common longing to be free of fear. We must not manipulate our people by playing upon their nightmares. We must serve mankind through genuine disarmament. With God's help we can secure life and freedom for generations to come.

Thank you very much.

12

Arms Reduction and Nuclear Deterrence

President Reagan wanted to update the American people on his efforts to achieve a lasting world peace. In his view, by following a prudent policy, the risk of nuclear conflict would be reduced and by maintaining a strong deterrent, the Soviets would be very unlikely to launch an attack. However, he underscored the increase in spending on defense by the Soviet Union compared to the U.S.

Reagan stressed, "We must replace and modernize our forces." To that end, he called for the production and deployment of the new ICBM known as the MX. Reagan also explained that, despite earlier talks with the Soviets, the Soviets were increasing their military strength. Reagan also said he was sending letters to the Soviet leadership proposing the two countries notify the other in advance of any major military exercises or launch of any intercontinental ballistic missiles.

Address to the Nation

November 22, 1982

Good evening.

The week before last was an especially moving one here in Washington. The Vietnam veterans finally came home once and for all to America's heart. They were welcomed with tears, with pride, and with a monument to their great sacrifice. Many of their names, like those of our republic's greatest citizens, are now engraved in stone in this city that belongs to all of us. On behalf of the nation, let me again thank the Vietnam veterans from the bottom of my heart for their courageous service to America.

Seeing those moving scenes, I know mothers of a new generation must have worried about their children and about peace. And that's what I'd like to talk to you about tonight—the future of our children in a world where peace is made uneasy by the presence of nuclear weapons.

A year ago, I said the time was right to move forward on arms control. I outlined several proposals and said nothing would have a higher priority in this administration. Now, a year later, I want to report on those proposals and on other efforts we're making to ensure the safety of our children's future.

The prevention of conflict and the reduction of weapons are the most important public issues of our time. Yet on no other issue are there more misconceptions and misunderstandings. You, the American people, deserve an explanation from your government on what our policy is on these issues. Too often, the experts have been content to discuss grandiose strategies among themselves and cloud the public debate in technicalities no one can understand. The result is that many Americans have become

frightened, and, let me say, fear of the unknown is entirely understandable. Unfortunately, much of the information emerging in
this debate bears little semblance to the facts.

To begin, let's go back to what the world was like at the end of
World War II. The United States was the only undamaged industrial power in the world. Our military power was at its peak, and
we alone had the atomic weapon. But we didn't use this wealth
and this power to bully; we used it to rebuild. We raised up the
war-ravaged economies, including the economies of those who
had fought against us. At first, the peace of the world was un-
threatened, because we alone were left with any real power and
we were using it for the good of our fellow man. Any potential
enemy was deterred from aggression because the cost would have
far outweighed the gain.

As the Soviets' power grew, we still managed to maintain the
peace. The United States had established a system of alliances,
with NATO as the centerpiece. In addition, we grew even more
respected as a world leader with a strong economy and deeply
held moral values.

With our commitment to help shape a better world, the United
States also pursued, and always pursued, every diplomatic channel for peace. And for at least thirty years after World War II, the
United States still continued to possess a large military advantage
over the Soviet Union. Our strength deterred—that is, prevented—aggression against us.

This nation's military objective has always been to maintain
peace by preventing war. This is neither a Democratic nor a Republican policy. It is supported by our allies and, most important
of all, it's worked for nearly forty years.

What do we mean when we speak of "nuclear deterrence"? Certainly, we don't want such weapons for their own sake. We don't
desire excessive forces or what some people have called "overkill."
Basically, it's a matter of others knowing that starting a conflict
would be more costly to them than anything they might hope to

gain. And, yes, it is sadly ironic that in these modern times it still takes weapons to prevent war. I wish it did not.

We desire peace. But peace is a goal, not a policy. Lasting peace is what we hope for at the end of our journey; it doesn't describe the steps we must take nor the paths we should follow to reach that goal.

I intend to search for peace along two parallel paths: deterrence and arms reductions. I believe these are the only paths that offer any real hope for an enduring peace.

And let me say, I believe that if we follow prudent policies, the risk of nuclear conflict will be reduced. Certainly, the United States will never use its forces except in response to attack. Through the years, Soviet leaders have also expressed a sober view of nuclear war. And if we maintain a strong deterrent, they are exceedingly unlikely to launch an attack.

Now, while the policy of deterrence has stood the test of time, the things we must do in order to maintain deterrence have changed. You often hear that the United States and the Soviet Union are in an arms race. Well, the truth is that while the Soviet Union has raced, we have not. As you can see from this blue U.S. line, in constant dollars, our defense spending in the 1960s went up because of Vietnam. And then it went downward through much of the 1970s. And now follow the red line, which is Soviet spending. It's gone up and up and up. In spite of a stagnating Soviet economy, Soviet leaders invest twelve to fourteen percent of their country's gross national product in military spending—two to three times the level we invest.

I might add that the defense share of our United States federal budget has gone way down, too. Watch the blue line again. In 1962, when John Kennedy was president, forty-six percent, almost half of the federal budget, went to our national defense. In recent years, about one quarter of our budget has gone to defense, while the share for social programs has nearly doubled. And most of our defense budget is spent on people, not weapons.

The combination of the Soviets spending more and the United States spending proportionately less changed the military balance and weakened our deterrent. Today, in virtually every measure of military power, the Soviet Union enjoys a decided advantage.

This chart shows the changes in the total number of international missiles and bombers. You will see that in 1962 and in 1972, the United States forces remained about the same—even dropping some by 1982. But take a look now at the Soviet side. In 1962, at the time of the Cuban missile crisis, the Soviets could not compare with us in terms of strength. In 1972, when we signed the SALT I treaty, we were nearly equal. But in 1982—well, that red Soviet bar stretching above the blue American bar tells the story.

I could show you chart after chart where there's a great deal of red and a much lesser amount of U.S. blue. For example, the Soviet Union has developed a third more land-based international ballistic missiles than we have. Believe it or not, we froze our number in 1965 and have deployed no additional missiles since then.

The Soviet Union put to sea sixty new ballistic-missile submarines in the last fifteen years. Until last year, we hadn't commissioned one in that same period.

The Soviet Union has built over 200 modern Backfire bombers and is building thirty more a year. For twenty years, the United States has deployed no new strategic bombers. Many of our B-52 bombers are now older than the pilots who fly them.

The Soviet Union now has 600 of the missiles considered most threatening by both sides—the intermediate-range missiles based on land. We have none. The United States withdrew its intermediate-range land-based missiles from Europe almost twenty years ago.

The world has also witnessed unprecedented growth in the area of Soviet conventional forces. The Soviets far exceed us in the number of tanks, artillery pieces, aircraft and ships they produce every year. What is more, when I arrived in this office. I learned that in our own forces we had planes that couldn't fly and ships that couldn't leave port mainly for lack of spare parts and crewmembers.

The Soviet military buildup must not be ignored. We've recognized the problem and, together with our allies, we've begun to correct the imbalance. Look at this chart of projected real defense spending for the next several years. Here is the Soviet line. Let us assume the Soviets' rate of spending remains at the level they've followed since the 1960s. The blue line is the United States. If my defense proposals are passed, it will still take five years before we come close to the Soviet level. Yet the modernization of our strategic and conventional forces will assure that deterrence works and peace prevails.

Our deployed nuclear forces were built before the age of microcircuits. It's not right to ask our young men and women in uniform to maintain and operate such antiques. Many have already given their lives to missile explosions and aircraft accidents caused by the old age of their equipment. We must replace and modernize our forces, and that's why I decided to proceed with the production and deployment of the new ICBM known as the MX.

Three earlier presidents worked to develop this missile. Based on the best advice that I could get, I concluded that the MX is the right missile at the right time. On the other hand, when I arrived in office I felt the proposal on where and how to base the missile simply cost too much in terms of money and the impact on our citizens' lives. I've concluded, however, it's absolutely essential that we proceed to produce this missile and that we base it in a series of closely based silos at Warren Air Force Base, near Cheyenne, Wyoming.

This plan requires only half as many missiles as the earlier plan and will fit in an area of only twenty square miles. It is the product of around-the-clock research that has been under way since I directed a search for a better, cheaper way. I urge the members of

Congress who must pass this plan to listen and examine the facts before they come to their own conclusion.

Some may question what modernizing our military has to do with peace. Well, as I explained earlier, a secure force keeps others from threatening us, and that keeps the peace. And just as important, it also increases the prospects of reaching significant arms reductions with the Soviets, and that's what we really want.

The United States wants deep cuts in the world's arsenal of weapons, but unless we demonstrate the will to rebuild our strength and restore the military balance, the Soviets, since they're so far ahead, have little incentive to negotiate with us.

Let me repeat that point, because it goes to the heart of our policies. Unless we demonstrate the will to rebuild our strength, the Soviets have little incentive to negotiate. If we hadn't begun to modernize, the Soviet negotiators would know we had nothing to bargain with except talk. They would know we were bluffing without a good hand, because they know what cards we hold just as we know what's in their hand.

You may recall that in 1969 the Soviets didn't want to negotiate a treaty banning anti-ballistic missiles. it was only after our Senate narrowly voted to fund an antiballistic missile program that the Soviets agreed to negotiate. We then reached an agreement. We also know that one-sided arms control doesn't work. We've tried time and time again to set an example by cutting our own forces in the hope that the Soviets would do likewise. The result has always been that they keep building.

I believe our strategy for peace will succeed. Never before has the United States proposed such a comprehensive program of nuclear arms control. Never in our history have we engaged in so many negotiations with the Soviets to reduce nuclear arms and to find a stable peace. What we are saying to them is this: We will modernize our military in order to keep the balance for peace, but wouldn't it be better if we both simply reduced our arsenals to a much lower level?

Let me begin with the negotiations on the intermediate-range nuclear forces that are currently under way in Geneva. As I said earlier, the most threatening of these forces are the land-based missiles which the Soviet Union now has aimed at Europe, the Middle East, and Asia.

This chart shows the number of warheads on these Soviet missiles. In 1972 there were 600. The United States was at zero. In 1977 there were 600. The United States was still at zero. Then the Soviets began deploying powerful new missiles with three warheads and a reach of thousands of miles—the SS-20. Since then, the bar has gone through the roof—the Soviets have added a missile with three warheads every week. Still, you see no United States blue on the chart. Although the Soviet leaders earlier this year declared they'd frozen deployment of this dangerous missile, they have in fact continued deployment.

Last year, on November 18, I proposed the total, global elimination of all these missiles. I proposed that the United States would deploy no comparable missiles, which are scheduled for late 1983, if the Soviet Union would dismantle theirs. We would follow agreement on the land-based missiles with limits on other intermediate-range systems.

The European governments strongly support our initiative. The Soviet Union has thus far shown little inclination to take this major step to zero levels. Yet I believe, and I'm hoping, that as the talks proceed and as we approach the scheduled placement of our new systems in Europe, the Soviet leaders will see the benefits of such a far-reaching agreement.

This summer we also began negotiations on strategic arms reductions, the proposal we call START. Here we're talking about intercontinental missiles, the weapons with a longer range than the intermediate-range ones I was just discussing. We're negotiating on the basis of deep reductions. I proposed in May that we cut the number of warheads on these missiles to an equal number, roughly one-third below current levels. I also proposed that we cut the number of missiles themselves to an equal number, about half the current U.S. level. Our proposals would eliminate some 4,700 warheads and some 2,250 missiles. I think that would be quite a service to mankind.

This chart shows the current level of United States ballistic missiles, both land- and sea-based. This is the Soviet level. We intend to convince the Soviets it would be in their own best interest to reduce these missiles. Look at the reduced numbers both sides would have under our proposal—quite a dramatic change. We also seek to reduce the total destructive power of these missiles and other elements of United States and Soviet strategic forces.

In 1977, when the last administration proposed more limited reductions, the Soviet Union refused even to discuss them. This time their reaction has been quite different. Their opening position is a serious one, and even though it doesn't meet our objective of deep reductions, there's no question we're heading in the right direction. One reason for this change is clear: the Soviet Union knows that we are now serious about our own strategic programs and that they must be prepared to negotiate in earnest.

We also have other important arms control efforts under way. In the talks in Vienna on mutual and balanced force reduction, we've proposed cuts in military personnel to a far lower and equal level. And in the forty-nation Committee on Disarmament in Geneva, we're working to develop effective limitations on nuclear testing and chemical weapons. The whole world remains outraged by the Soviets and their allies' use of biological and chemical weapons against defenseless people in Afghanistan, Cambodia and Laos. This experience makes ironclad verification all the more essential for arms control.

There is, of course, much more that needs to be done. In an age when intercontinental missiles can span half the globe in less than half an hour, it's crucial that Soviet and American leaders have clear understanding of each other's capabilities and intentions.

Last June in Berlin, and again at the United Nations Special Session on Disarmament, I vowed that the United States would make every effort to reduce the risks of accident and misunderstanding and thus to strengthen mutual confidence between the United States and the Soviet Union. Since then, we've been actively studying detailed measures to implement this Berlin initiative.

Today I would like to announce some of the measures which I've proposed in a special letter just sent to the Soviet leadership and which I've instructed our ambassadors in Geneva to discuss with their Soviet counterparts. They include, but also go beyond, some of the suggestions I made in Berlin.

The first of these measures involves advance notification of all United States and Soviet test launches of intercontinental ballistic missiles. We will also seek Soviet agreement on notification of all sea-launched ballistic missiles as well as intermediate-range land-based ballistic missiles of the type we're currently negotiating. This would remove surprise and uncertainty at the sudden appearance of such missiles on the warning screens of the two countries.

In another area of potential misunderstanding, we propose to the Soviets that we provide each other with advance notification of our major military exercises. Here again, our objective is to reduce the surprise and uncertainty surrounding otherwise sudden moves by either side.

These sorts of measures are designed to deal with the immediate issues of miscalculation in time of crisis. But there are deeper, longer-term problems as well. In order to clear away some of the mutual ignorance and suspicion between our two countries, I will propose that we both engage in broad-ranging exchange of basic data about our nuclear forces. I am instructing our ambassadors at the negotiations on both strategic and intermediate forces to seek Soviet agreement on an expanded exchange of information. The more one side knows about what the other side is doing, the less room there is for surprise and miscalculation.

Probably everyone has heard of the so-called hot line which enables me to communicate directly with the Soviet leadership in the event of a crisis. The existing hot line is dependable and rapid, with both ground and satellite links. But because it's so important, I've also directed that we carefully examine any possible improvements to the existing hot line system.

Now, although we've begun negotiations on these many proposals, this doesn't mean we've exhausted all the initiatives that could help to reduce the risk of accidental conflict. We'll leave no opportunity unexplored, and we'll consult closely with Senators Nunn, Jackson and Warner, and other members of the Congress who have made important suggestions in this field.

We're also making strenuous efforts to prevent the spread of nuclear weapons to additional countries. It would be tragic if we succeeded in reducing existing arsenals only to have new threats emerge in other areas of the world.

Earlier, I spoke of America's contributions to peace following World War II, of all we did to promote peace and prosperity for our fellow man. Well, we're still those same people. We still seek peace above all else.

I want to remind our own citizens and those around the world of this tradition of American good will, because I am concerned about the effects the nuclear fear is having on our people. The most upsetting letters I receive are from schoolchildren who write to me as a class assignment. It's evident they've discussed the most nightmarish aspects of a nuclear holocaust in their classrooms. Their letters are often full of terror. Well, this should not be so.

The philosopher Spinoza said, "Peace is a virtue, a state of mind, a disposition for benevolence, confidence, justice." Well, those are the qualities we want our children to inherit—not fear. They must grow up confident if they're to meet the challenges of tomorrow as we will meet the challenges of today.

I began these remarks speaking of our children. I want to close on the same theme. Our children should not grow up frightened.

They should not fear the future. We're working to make it peaceful and free. I believe their future can be the brightest, most exciting of any generation. We must reassure them and let them know that their parents and the leaders of this world are seeking, above all else, to keep them safe and at peace. I consider this to be a sacred trust.

My fellow Americans, on this Thanksgiving when we have so much to be grateful for, let us give special thanks for our peace, our freedom, and our good people.

I've always believed that this land was set aside in an uncommon way, that a Divine plan placed this great continent between the oceans to be found by a people from every corner of the earth who had a special love of faith, freedom and peace.

Let us reaffirm America's destiny of goodness and good will. Let us work for peace and, as we do, let us remember the lines of the famous old hymn: "O God of Love, O King of Peace, make wars throughout the world to cease."

Thank you. Good night, and God bless you.

13

"THE EVIL EMPIRE"

This speech has been called, by historians, politicians, and other observers, the most important one of the Reagan administration. The president bluntly described the fight with the Soviets observing, "The Soviet leaders have openly and publicly declared that the only morality they recognize is that which will further their cause, which is world revolution." In fact, it is these comments that prompted some people in Poland and East Berlin to greet the President as a hero when he visited there not long after this speech. Responding directly to those who were calling for a nuclear freeze, he said, "The truth is that a freeze now would be a very dangerous fraud, for that is merely the illusion of peace." In fact, the speechwriter Anthony Dolan had tried on several previous times to use the phrase "evil empire" in speeches but the State Department had always removed the saying. This time, however, Reagan kept it in.

Address to the National Association of Evangelicals, Orlando, Florida

MARCH 8, 1983

———

Reverend, clergy, Senator Hawkins, distinguished members of the Florida congressional delegation, and all of you:

I can't tell you how you have warmed my heart with your welcome. I'm delighted to be here today.

Those of you in the National Association of Evangelicals are known for your spiritual and humanitarian work. And I would be especially remiss if I didn't discharge right now one personal debt of gratitude. Thank you for your prayers. Nancy and I have felt their presence many times in many ways. And believe me, for us they've made all the difference.

The other day in the East Room of the White House at a meeting there, someone asked me whether I was aware of all the people out there who were praying for the president. And I had to say, "Yes, I am. I've felt it. I believe in intercessionary prayer." But I couldn't help but say to that questioner after he'd asked the question, that—or at least say to them that—if sometimes when he was praying he got a busy signal, it was just me in there ahead of him. [Laughter] I think I understand how Abraham Lincoln felt when he said, "I have been driven many times to my knees by the overwhelming conviction that I had nowhere else to go."

From the joy and the good feeling of this conference, I go to a political reception. [Laughter] Now, I don't know why, but that bit of scheduling reminds me of a story—which I'll share with you.

An evangelical minister and a politician arrived at Heaven's gate one day together. And St. Peter, after doing all the necessary formalities, took them in hand to show them where their quarters would be. And he took them to a small single room with a bed, a chair and a table and said this was for the clergyman. And the politician was a little worried about what might be in store for him. And he couldn't believe it, then, when St. Peter stopped in front of a beautiful mansion with lovely grounds, many servants, and told him that these would be his quarters.

And he couldn't help but ask. He said, "But wait, how—there's something wrong—how do I get this mansion while that good and holy man only gets a single room?" And St. Peter said, "You have to understand how things are up here. We've got thousands and thousands of clergy. You're the first politician who ever made it." [Laughter]

But I don't want to contribute to a stereotype. [Laughter] So, I tell you there are a great many God-fearing, dedicated, noble men and women in public life, present company included. And, yes, we need your help to keep us ever mindful of the ideas and the principles that brought us into the public arena in the first place. The basis of those ideals and principles is a commitment to freedom and personal liberty that, itself, is grounded in the much deeper realization that freedom prospers only where the blessings of God are avidly sought and humbly accepted.

The American experiment in democracy rests on this insight. Its discovery was the great triumph of our Founding Fathers, voiced by William Penn when he said: "If we will not be governed by God, we must be governed by tyrants." Explaining the inalienable rights of men, Jefferson said, "The God who gave us life, gave us liberty at the same time." And it was George Washington who said that "of all the dispositions and habits which lead to political prosperity, religion and morality are indispensable supports."

And finally, that shrewdest of all observers of American democracy, Alexis de Tocqueville, put it eloquently after he had gone on a search for the secret of America's greatness and genius—and he said: "Not until I went into the churches of America and heard her pulpits aflame with righteousness did I understand the greatness and the genius of America. America is good, and if America ever ceases to be good, America will cease to be great."

Well, I'm pleased to be here today with you who are keeping America great by keeping her good. Only through your work and prayers and those of millions of others can we hope to survive this perilous century and keep alive this experiment in liberty, this last, best hope of man.

I want you to know that this administration is motivated by a political philosophy that sees the greatness of America in you, her people, and in your families, churches, neighborhoods, communities—the institutions that foster and nourish values like concern for others and respect for the rule of law under God.

Now, I don't have to tell you that this puts us in opposition to, or at least out of step with, a prevailing attitude of many who have turned to a modern-day secularism, discarding the tried and time-tested values upon which our very civilization is based. No matter how well-intentioned, their value system is radically different from that of most Americans. And while they proclaim that they're freeing us from superstitions of the past, they've taken upon themselves the job of superintending us by government rule and regulation. Sometimes their voices are louder than ours, but they are not yet a majority.

An example of that vocal superiority is evident in a controversy now going on in Washington. And since I'm involved, I've been waiting to hear from the parents of young America. How far are they willing to go in giving to government their prerogatives as parents?

Let me state the case as briefly and simply as I can. An organization of citizens, sincerely motivated and deeply concerned about the increase in illegitimate births and abortions involving girls well below the age of consent, some time ago established a nationwide network of clinics to offer help to these girls and, hopefully, alleviate this situation. Now, again, let me say I do not fault their intent. However, in their well-intentioned effort, these clinics have decided to provide advice and birth control drugs and devices to underage girls without the knowledge of their parents.

For some years now, the federal government has helped with funds to subsidize these clinics. In providing for this, the Congress decreed that every effort would be made to maximize parental participation. Nevertheless, the drugs and devices are prescribed without getting parental consent or giving notification after they've done so. Girls termed "sexually active"—and that has replaced the word "promiscuous"—are given this help in order to prevent illegitimate birth or abortion.

Well, we have ordered clinics receiving federal funds to notify the parents such help has been given. One of the nation's leading newspapers has created the term "squeal rule" in editorializing against us for doing this, and we're being criticized for violating the privacy of young people. A judge has recently granted an injunction against an enforcement of our rule. I've watched TV panel shows discuss this issue, seen columnists pontificating on our error, but no one seems to mention morality as playing a part in the subject of sex.

Is all of Judeo-Christian tradition wrong? Are we to believe that something so sacred can be looked upon as a purely physical thing with no potential for emotional and psychological harm? And isn't it the parents' right to give counsel and advice to keep their children from making mistakes that may affect their entire lives?

Many of us in government would like to know what parents think about this intrusion in their family by government. We're going to fight in the courts. The rights of parents and the rights of family take precedence over those of Washington-based bureaucrats and social engineers.

But the fight against parental notification is really only one example of many attempts to water down traditional values and even abrogate the original terms of American democracy. Freedom prospers when religion is vibrant and the rule of law under

God is acknowledged. When our Founding Fathers passed the First Amendment, they sought to protect churches from government interference. They never intended to construct a wall of hostility between government and the concept of religious belief itself.

The evidence of this permeates our history and our government. The Declaration of Independence mentions the Supreme Being no less than four times. "In God We Trust" is engraved on our coinage. The Supreme Court opens its proceedings with a religious invocation. And the members of Congress open their sessions with a prayer. I just happen to believe the schoolchildren of the United States are entitled to the same privileges as Supreme Court justices and congressmen.

Last year I sent the Congress a constitutional amendment to restore prayer to public schools. Already this session, there's growing bipartisan support for the amendment, and I am calling on the Congress to act speedily to pass it and to let our children pray.

Perhaps some of you read recently about the Lubbock school case, where a judge actually ruled that it was unconstitutional for a school district to give equal treatment to religious and nonreligious student groups, even when the group meetings were being held during the student's own time. The First Amendment never intended to require government to discriminate against religious speech.

Senators Denton and Hatfield have proposed legislation in the Congress on the whole question of prohibiting discrimination against religious forms of student speech. Such legislation could go far to restore freedom of religious speech for public school students. And I hope the Congress considers these bills quickly. And with your help, I think it's possible we could also get the constitutional amendment through the Congress this year.

More than a decade ago, a Supreme Court decision literally wiped off the books of fifty states statutes protecting the rights of unborn children. Abortion on demand now takes the lives of up to one and a half million unborn children a year. Human life legislation ending this tragedy will someday pass the Congress, and you and I must never rest until it does. Unless and until it can be proven that the unborn child is not a living entity, then its right to life, liberty and the pursuit of happiness must be protected.

You may remember that when abortion on demand began, many—and indeed, I'm sure many of you—warned that the practice would lead to a decline in respect for human life, that the philosophical premises used to justify abortion on demand would ultimately be used to justify other attacks on the sacredness of human life: infanticide or mercy killing. Tragically enough, those warnings proved all too true. Only last year a court permitted the death by starvation of a handicapped infant.

I have directed the Health and Human Services Department to make clear to every healthcare facility in the United States that the Rehabilitation Act of 1973 protects all handicapped persons against discrimination based on handicaps, including infants. And we have taken the further step of requiring that each and every recipient of federal funds who provides healthcare services to infants must post and keep posted in a conspicuous place a notice stating that "discriminatory failure to feed and care for handicapped infants in this facility is prohibited by federal law." It also lists a twenty-four-hour, toll-free number so that nurses and others may report violations in time to save the infant's life.

In addition, recent legislation introduced in the Congress by Representative Henry Hyde of Illinois not only increases restrictions on publicly financed abortions, it also addresses this whole problem of infanticide. I urge the Congress to begin hearings and to adopt legislation that will protect the right to life of all children, including the disabled or handicapped.

Now, I'm sure that you must get discouraged at times, but you've done better than you know, perhaps. There's a great spiritual awakening in America, a renewal of the traditional values that have been the bedrock of America's goodness and greatness.

One recent survey by a Washington-based research council concluded that Americans were far more religious than the people of other nations; ninety-five percent of those surveyed expressed a belief in God and a huge minority believed the Ten Commandments had real meaning in their lives. And another study has found that an overwhelming majority of Americans disapprove of adultery, teenage sex, pornography, abortion, and hard drugs. And this same study showed a deep reverence for the importance of family ties and religious belief.

I think the items that we've discussed here today must be a key part of the nation's political agenda. For the first time the Congress is openly and seriously debating and leading with the prayer and abortion issues—and that's enormous progress right there. I repeat: America is in the midst of a spiritual awakening and a moral renewal. And with your biblical keynote, I say today, "Yes, let justice roll on like a river, righteousness like a never-failing stream."

Now, obviously, much of this new political and social consensus I've talked about is based on a positive view of American history, one that takes pride in our country's accomplishments and record. But we must never forget that no government schemes are going to perfect man. We know that living in this world means dealing with what philosophers would call the phenomenology of evil, or, as theologians would put it, the doctrine of sin.

There is sin and evil in the world, and we're enjoined by Scripture and the Lord Jesus to oppose it with all our might. Our nation, too, has a legacy of evil with which it must deal. The glory of this land has been its capacity for transcending the moral evils of our past. For example, the long struggle of minority citizens for equal rights, once a source of disunity and civil war, is now a point of pride for all Americans. We must never go back. There is no room for racism, anti-Semitism, or other forms of ethnic and racial hatred in this country.

I know that you've been horrified, as have I, by the resurgence of some hate groups preaching bigotry and prejudice. Use the mighty voice of your pulpits and the powerful standing of your churches to denounce and isolate these hate groups in our midst. The commandment given us is clear and simple: "Thou shalt love thy neighbor as thyself."

But whatever sad episodes exist in our past, any objective observer must hold a positive view of American history, a history that has been the story of hopes fulfilled and dreams made into reality. Especially in this century, America has kept alight the torch of freedom, not just for ourselves but for millions of others around the world.

And this brings me to my final point today. During my first press conference as president, in answer to a direct question, I pointed out that, as good Marxist-Leninists, the Soviet leaders have openly and publicly declared that the only morality they recognize is that which will further their cause, which is world revolution. I think I should point out I was only quoting Lenin, their guiding spirit, who said in 1920 that they repudiate all morality that proceeds from supernatural ideas—that's their name for religion—or ideas that are outside class conceptions. Morality is entirely subordinate to the interests of class war. And everything is moral that is necessary for the annihilation of the old, exploiting social order and for uniting the proletariat.

Well, I think the refusal of many influential people to accept this elementary fact of Soviet doctrine illustrates an historical reluctance to see totalitarian powers for what they are. We saw this phenomenon in the 1930s. We see it too often today.

This doesn't mean we should isolate ourselves and refuse to seek an understanding with them. I intend to do everything I can to persuade them of our peaceful intent, to remind them that it was the West that refused to see its nuclear monopoly in the forties and fifties for territorial gain and which now proposes fifty percent cut in strategic ballistic missiles and the elimination of an entire class of land-based, intermediate-range nuclear missiles.

At the same time, however, they must be made to understand we will never compromise our principles and standards. We will never give away our freedom. We will never abandon our belief in God. And we will never stop searching for a genuine peace. But we can assure none of these things America stands for through the so-called nuclear freeze solutions proposed by some.

The truth is that a freeze now would be a very dangerous fraud, for that is merely the illusion of peace. The reality is that we must find peace through strength.

I would agree to a freeze if only we could freeze the Soviets' global desires. A freeze at current levels of weapons would remove any incentive for the Soviets to negotiate seriously in Geneva and virtually end our chances to achieve the major arms reductions which we have proposed. Instead, they would achieve their objectives through the freeze.

A freeze would reward the Soviet Union for its enormous and unparalleled military buildup. It would prevent the essential and long-overdue modernization of United States and allied defenses and would leave our aging forces increasingly vulnerable. And an honest freeze would require extensive prior negotiations on the systems and numbers to be limited and on the measures to ensure effective verification and compliance. And the kind of a freeze that has been suggested would be virtually impossible to verify. Such a major effort would divert us completely from our current negotiations on achieving substantial reductions.

A number of years ago, I heard a young father, a very prominent young man in the entertainment world, addressing a tremendous gathering in California. It was during the time of the Cold War, and Communism and our own way of life were very much on people's minds. And he was speaking to that subject. And suddenly, though, I heard him saying, "I love my little girls more than anything—" And I said to myself, "Oh, no, don't. You can't—don't say that." But I had underestimated him. He went on: "I would rather see my little girls die now, still believing in God, than have them grow up under Communism and one day die no longer believing in God."

There were thousands of young people in that audience. They came to their feet with shouts of joy. They had instantly recognized the profound truth in what he had said, with regard to the physical and the soul and what was truly important.

Yes, let us pray for the salvation of all of those who live in that totalitarian darkness—pray they will discover the joy of knowing God. But until they do, let us be aware that while they preach the supremacy of the state, declare its omnipotence over individual man, and predict its eventual domination of all peoples on the earth, they are the focus of evil in the modern world.

It was C. S. Lewis who, in his unforgettable *Screwtape Letters*, wrote: "The greatest evil is not done now in those sordid 'dens of crime' that Dickens loved to paint. It is not even done in concentration camps and labor camps. In those we see its final result. But it is conceived and ordered (moved, seconded, carried, and minuted) in clear, carpeted, warmed, and well-lighted offices, by quiet men with white collars and cut fingernails and smooth-shaven cheeks who do not need to raise their voice."

Well, because these "quiet men" do not "raise their voices," because they sometimes speak in soothing tones of brotherhood and peace, because, like other dictators before them, they're always making "their final territorial demand," some would have us accept them at their word and accommodate ourselves to their aggressive impulses. But if history teaches anything, it teaches that simple-minded appeasement or wishful thinking about our adversaries is folly. It means the betrayal of our past, the squandering of our freedom.

So, I urge you to speak out against those who would place the United States in a position of military and moral inferiority. You know, I've always believed that old Screwtape reserved his best efforts for those of you in the church. So, in your discussions of the nuclear freeze proposals, I urge you to beware the temptation of pride—the temptation of blithely declaring yourselves above it all and label both sides equally at fault, to ignore the facts of history and the aggressive impulses of an evil empire, to simply call the arms race a giant misunderstanding and thereby remove yourself from the struggle between right and wrong and good and evil.

I ask you to resist the attempts of those who would have you withhold your support for our efforts, this administration's efforts, to keep America strong and free, while we negotiate real and verifiable reductions in the world's nuclear arsenals and one day, with God's help, their total elimination.

While America's military strength is important, let me add here that I've always maintained that the struggle now going on for the world will never be decided by bombs or rockets, by armies or military might. The real crisis we face today is a spiritual one; at root, it is a test of moral will and faith.

Whittaker Chambers, the man whose own religious conversion made him a witness to one of the terrible traumas of our time, the Hiss-Chambers case, wrote that the crisis of the Western World exists to the degree in which the West is indifferent to God, the degree to which it collaborates in Communism's attempt to make man stand alone without God. And then he said, "for Marxism-Leninism is actually the second oldest faith, first proclaimed in the Garden of Eden with the worlds of temptation, 'Ye shall be as gods.'"

The Western World can answer this challenge, he wrote, "but only provided that its faith in God and the freedom He enjoins is as great as Communism's faith in Man."

I believe we shall rise to the challenge. I believe that Communism is another sad, bizarre chapter in human history whose last pages even now are being written. I believe this because the source of our strength in the quest for human freedom is not material, but spiritual. And because it knows no limitation, it must terrify and ultimately triumph over those who would enslave their fellow man. For in the words of Isaiah: "He giveth power to the faint; and to them that have no might He increased strength. But they that wait upon the Lord shall renew their strength; they shall mount up with wings as eagles; they shall run, and not be weary."

Yes, change your world. One of our Founding Fathers, Thomas Paine, said, "We have it within our power to begin the world over again." We can do it, doing together what no one church could do by itself.

God bless you, and thank you very much.

14

AMERICA NEEDS MISSILE DEFENSE

This address proved to be one of the most discussed of the Reagan administration. Reagan made his case directly to the public announcing the Strategic Defense Initiative (SDI) without consulting Congress. He described a system that would enable the U.S. to intercept and disarm any long range ballistic missiles that carried weapons of mass destruction. This billion dollar-plus plan would link land, sea, air, and space-based weapons with one communications system. In his words, "What if free people could live secure in the knowledge that their security did not rest upon the threat of instant U.S. retaliation to deter a Soviet attack, that we could intercept and destroy strategic ballistic missiles before they reached our own soil or that of our allies." Despite criticism, the work on SDI continued to the end of his administration and through President George Bush's tenure as well.

Address to the Nation

March 23, 1983

––––––

My fellow Americans, thank you for sharing your time with me tonight.

The subject I want to discuss with you, peace and national security, is both timely and important. Timely, because I've reached a decision which offers a new hope for our children in the twenty-first century, a decision I'll tell you about in a few minutes. And important because there's a very big decision that you must make for yourselves. This subject involves the most basic duty that any president and any people share, the duty to protect and strengthen the peace.

At the beginning of this year, I submitted to the Congress a defense budget which reflects my best judgment of the best understanding of the experts and specialists who advise me about what we and our allies must do to protect our people in the years ahead. That budget is much more than a long list of numbers, for behind all the numbers lies America's ability to prevent the greatest of human tragedies and preserve our free way of life in a sometimes dangerous world. It is part of a careful, long-term plan to make America strong again after too many years of neglect and mistakes.

Our efforts to rebuild America's defenses and strengthen the peace began two years ago when we requested a major increase in the defense program. Since then, the amount of those increases we first proposed has been reduced by half, through improvements in management and procurement and other savings.

The budget request that is now before the Congress has been trimmed to the limits of safety. Further deep cuts cannot be made without seriously endangering the security of the nation. The choice is up to the men and women you've elected to the Congress, and that means the choice is up to you.

Tonight I want to explain to you what this defense debate is all about and why I'm convinced that the budget now before the Congress is necessary, responsible, and deserving of your support. And I want to offer hope for the future.

But first, let me say what the defense debate is not about. It is not about spending arithmetic. I know that in the last few weeks you've been bombarded with numbers and percentages. Some say we need only a five percent increase in defense spending. The so-called alternate budget backed by liberals in the House of Representatives would lower the figure to two to three percent, cutting our defense spending by $163 billion over the next five years. The trouble with all these numbers is that they tell us little about the kind of defense program America needs or the benefits and security and freedom that our defense effort buys for us.

What seems to have been lost in all this debate is the simple truth of how a defense budget is arrived at. It isn't done by deciding to spend a certain number of dollars. Those loud voices that are occasionally heard charging that the government is trying to solve a security problem by throwing money at it are nothing more than noise based on ignorance. We start by considering what must be done to maintain peace and review all the possible threats against our security. Then a strategy for strengthening peace and defending against those threats must be agreed upon. And, finally, our defense establishment must be evaluated to see what is necessary to protect against any or all of the potential threats. The cost of achieving these ends is totaled up, and the result is the budget for national defense.

There is no logical way that you can say, let's spend x billion dollars less. You can only say, which part of our defense measures do we believe we can do without and still have security against all contingencies? Anyone in the Congress who advocates a percentage or a specific dollar cut in defense spending should be made to say what part of our defenses he would eliminate, and he should be candid enough to acknowledge that his cuts mean cutting our commitments to allies or inviting greater risk or both.

The defense policy of the United States is based on a simple premise: The United States does not start fights. We will never be an aggressor. We maintain our strength in order to deter and defend against aggression—to preserve freedom and peace.

Since the dawn of the atomic age, we've sought to reduce the risk of war by maintaining a strong deterrent and by seeking genuine arms control. "Deterrence" means simply this: making sure any adversary who thinks about attacking the United States, or our allies, or our vital interests, concludes that the risks to him outweigh any potential gains. Once he understands that, he won't attack. We maintain the peace through our strength; weakness only invites aggression.

This strategy of deterrence has not changed. It still works. But what it takes to maintain deterrence has changed. It took one kind of military force to deter an attack when we had far more nuclear weapons than any other power; it takes another kind now that the Soviets, for example, have enough accurate and powerful nuclear weapons to destroy virtually all of our missiles on the ground. Now, this is not to say that the Soviet Union is planning to make war on us. Nor do I believe a war is inevitable—quite the contrary. But what must be recognized is that our security is based on being prepared to meet all threats.

There was a time when we depended on coastal forts and artillery batteries, because, with the weaponry of that day, any attack would have had to come by sea. Well, this is a different world, and our defenses must be based on recognition and awareness of the weaponry possessed by other nations in the nuclear age.

We can't afford to believe that we will never be threatened. There have been two world wars in my lifetime. We didn't start them and, indeed, did everything we could to avoid being drawn into them. But we were ill-prepared for both. Had we been better prepared, peace might have been preserved.

For twenty years the Soviet Union has been accumulating enormous military might. They didn't stop when their forces exceeded all requirements of a legitimate defensive capability. And they haven't stopped now. During the past decade and a half, the Soviets have built up a massive arsenal of new strategic nuclear weapons—weapons that can strike directly at the United States.

As an example, the United States introduced its last new intercontinental ballistic missile, the Minute Man III, in 1969, and we're now dismantling our even older Titan missiles. But what has the Soviet Union done in these intervening years? Well, since 1969 the Soviet Union has built five new classes of ICBMs and upgraded these eight times. As a result, their missiles are much more powerful and accurate than they were several years ago, and they continue to develop more, while ours are increasingly obsolete.

The same thing has happened in other areas. Over the same period, the Soviet Union built four new classes of submarine-launched ballistic missiles and over sixty new missile submarines. We built two new types of submarine missiles and actually withdrew ten submarines from strategic missions. The Soviet Union built over 200 new Backfire bombers, and their brand-new Blackjack bomber is now under development. We haven't built a new long-range bomber since our B-52s were deployed about a quarter of a century ago, and we've already retired several hundred of those because of old age. Indeed, despite what many people think, our strategic forces only cost about fifteen percent of the defense budget.

Another example of what's happened: in 1978 the Soviets had 600 intermediate-range nuclear missiles based on land and were beginning to add the SS-20—a new, highly accurate, mobile missile with three warheads. We had none. Since then the Soviets have strengthened their lead. By the end of 1979, when Soviet leader Brezhnev declared "a balance now exists," the Soviets had over 800 warheads. We still had none. A year ago this month, Mr. Brezhnev pledged a moratorium, or freeze, on SS-20 deployment. But by last August, their 800 warheads had become more than 1,200. We still had none. Some freeze. At this time, Soviet Defense Minister Ustinov announced "approximate parity of forces continues to exist." But the Soviets are still adding an average of three new warheads a week and now have 1,300. These warheads can reach their targets in a matter of a few minutes. We still have none. So far, it seems that the Soviet definition of parity is a box score of 1,300 to nothing, in their favor.

So, together with our NATO allies, we decided in 1979 to deploy new weapons, beginning this year, as a deterrent to their SS-20s and as an incentive to the Soviet Union to meet us in serious arms control negotiations. We will begin that deployment late this year. At the same time, however, we're willing to cancel our program if the Soviets will dismantle theirs. This is what we've called a zero-zero plan. The Soviets are now at the negotiating table—and I think it's fair to say that without our planned deployments, they wouldn't be there.

Now let's consider conventional forces. Since 1974 the United States has produced 3,050 tactical combat aircraft. By contrast, the Soviet Union has produced twice as many. When we look at attack submarines, the United States has produced twenty-seven while the Soviet Union has produced sixty-one. For armored vehicles, including tanks, we have produced 11,200. The Soviet Union has produced 54,000—nearly five to one in their favor. Finally, with artillery, we've produced 950 artillery and rocket launchers while the Soviets have produced more than 13,000—a staggering fourteen-to-one ratio.

There was a time when we were able to offset superior Soviet numbers with higher quality, but today they are building weapons as sophisticated and modern as our own.

As the Soviets have increased their military power, they've been emboldened to extend that power. They're spreading their military influence in ways that can directly challenge our vital interests and those of our allies.

The following aerial photographs, most of them secret until now, illustrate this point in a crucial area very close to home: Central America and the Caribbean Basin. They're not dramatic photographs, but I think they help give you a better understanding of what I'm talking about.

This Soviet intelligence collection facility, less than a hundred miles from our coast, is the largest of its kind in the world. The acres and acres of antennae fields and intelligence monitors are targeted on key U.S. military installations and sensitive activities. The installation in Lourdes, Cuba, is manned by 1,500 Soviet technicians. And the satellite ground station allows instant communications with Moscow. This twenty-eight-square-mile facility has grown by more than sixty percent in size and capability during the past decade.

In western Cuba, we see this military airfield and its complement of modern, Soviet-built Mig-23 aircraft. The Soviet Union uses this Cuban airfield for its own long-range reconnaissance missions. And earlier this month, two modern Soviet anti-submarine warfare aircraft began operating from it. During the past two years, the level of Soviet arms exports to Cuba can only be compared to the levels reached during the Cuban missile crisis twenty years ago.

This third photo, which is the only one in this series that has been previously made public, shows Soviet military hardware that has made its way to Central America. This airfield, with its Ml-8 helicopters, anti-aircraft guns, and protected fighter sites, is one of a number of military facilities in Nicaragua which has received Soviet equipment funneled through Cuba, and reflects the massive military buildup going on in that country.

On the small island of Grenada, at the southern end of the Caribbean chain, the Cubans, with Soviet financing and backing, are in the process of building an airfield with a 10,000-foot runway.

Grenada doesn't even have an air force. Who is it intended for? The Caribbean is a very important passageway for our international commerce and military lines of communication. More than half of all American oil imports now pass through the Caribbean. The rapid buildup of Grenada's military potential is unrelated to any conceivable threat to this island country of under 110,000 people and totally at odds with the pattern of other eastern Caribbean states, most of which are unarmed.

The Soviet-Cuban militarization of Grenada, in short, can only be seen as power projection into the region. And it is in this important economic and strategic area that we're trying to help the governments of El Salvador, Costa Rica, Honduras, and others in their struggles for democracy against guerrillas supported through Cuba and Nicaragua.

These pictures only tell a small part of the story. I wish I could show you more without compromising our most sensitive intelligence sources and methods. But the Soviet Union is also supporting Cuban military forces in Angola and Ethiopia. They have bases in Ethiopia and South Yemen, near the Persian Gulf oil fields. They've taken over the port that we built at Cam Ranh Bay in Vietnam. And now, for the first time in history, the Soviet navy is a force to be reckoned with in the South Pacific.

Some people may still ask: Would the Soviets ever use their formidable military power? Well, again, can we afford to believe they won't? There is Afghanistan. And in Poland, the Soviets denied the will of the people and in so doing demonstrated to the world how their military power could also be used to intimidate.

The final fact is that the Soviet Union is acquiring what can only be considered an offensive military force. They have continued to build far more intercontinental ballistic missiles than they could possibly need simply to deter an attack. Their conventional forces are trained and equipped not so much to defend against an attack as they are to permit sudden, surprise offensives of their own.

Our NATO allies have assumed a great defense burden, including the military draft in most countries. We're working with them and our other friends around the world to do more. Our defensive strategy means we need military forces that can move very quickly, forces that are trained and ready to respond to any emergency.

Every item in our defense program—our ships, our tanks, our planes, our funds for training and spare parts—is intended for one all-important purpose: to keep the peace. Unfortunately, a decade of neglecting our military forces has called into question our ability to do that.

When I took office in January 1981, I was appalled by what I found: American planes that couldn't fly and American ships that couldn't sail for lack of spare parts and trained personnel and insufficient fuel and ammunition for essential training. The inevitable result of all this was poor morale in our armed forces, difficulty in recruiting the brightest young Americans to wear the uniform, and difficulty in convincing our most experienced military personnel to stay on.

There was a real question then about how well we could meet a crisis. And it was obvious that we had to begin a major modernization program to ensure we could deter aggression and preserve the peace in the years ahead.

We had to move immediately to improve the basic readiness and staying power of our conventional forces, so they could meet—and therefore help deter—a crisis. We had to make up for lost years of investment by moving forward with a long-term plan to prepare our forces to counter the military capabilities our adversaries were developing for the future.

I know that all of you want peace, and so do I. I know, too, that many of you seriously believe that a nuclear freeze would further the cause of peace. But a freeze now would make us less, not more, secure and would raise, not reduce, the risks of war. It would be largely unverifiable and would seriously undercut our negotiations on arms reduction. It would reward the Soviets for their massive military buildup while preventing us from modernizing our aging and increasingly vulnerable forces. With their present margin of superiority, why should they agree to arms reductions knowing that we were prohibited from catching up?

Believe me, it wasn't pleasant for someone who had come to Washington determined to reduce government spending, but we had to move forward with the task of repairing our defenses or we would lose our ability to deter conflict now and in the future. We had to demonstrate to any adversary that aggression could not succeed and that the only real solution was substantial, equitable, and effectively verifiable arms reduction—the kind we're working for right now in Geneva.

Thanks to your strong support, and bipartisan support from the Congress, we began to turn things around. Already we're seeing some very encouraging results. Quality recruitment and retention are up dramatically—more high school graduates are choosing military careers, and more experienced career personnel are choosing to stay. Our men and women in uniform at last are getting the tools and training they need to do their jobs.

Ask around today, especially among our young people, and I think you will find a whole new attitude toward serving their country. This reflects more than just better pay, equipment, and leadership. You, the American people, have sent a signal to these young people that it is once again an honor to wear the uniform. That's not something you measure in a budget, but it's a very real part of our nation's strength.

It will take us longer to build the kind of equipment we need to keep peace in the future, but we've made a good start.

We haven't built a new long-range bomber for twenty-one years. Now we're building the B-1. We hadn't launched one new strategic submarine for seventeen years. Now we're building one Trident submarine a year. Our land-based missiles are increasingly threatened by the many huge, new Soviet ICBMs. We're determining how to solve that problem. At the same time, we're working in the START and INF negotiations with the goal of achieving deep reductions in the strategic and intermediate nuclear arsenals of both sides.

We have also begun the long-needed modernization of our conventional forces. The Army is getting its first new tank in twenty years. The Air Force is modernizing. We're rebuilding our Navy, which shrank from about a thousand ships in the late 1960s to 453 during the 1970s. Our nation needs a superior navy to support our military forces and vital interests overseas. We're now on the road to achieving a 600-ship Navy and increasing the amphibious capabilities of our Marines, who are now serving the cause of peace in Lebanon. And we're building a real capability to assist our friends in the vitally important Indian Ocean and Persian Gulf region.

This adds up to a major effort, and it isn't cheap. It comes at a time when there are many other pressures on our budget and when the American people have already had to make major sacrifices during the recession. But we must not be misled by those who would make defense once again the scapegoat of the federal budget.

The fact is that in the past few decades we have seen a dramatic shift in how we spend the taxpayer's dollar. Back in 1955, payments to individuals took up only about twenty percent of the federal budget. For nearly three decades, these payments steadily increased and this year will account for forty-nine percent of the budget. By contrast, in 1955 defense took up more than half of the federal budget. By 1980 this spending had fallen to a low of twenty-three percent. Even with the increase that I am requesting this year, defense will still amount to only twenty-eighty percent of the budget.

The calls for cutting back the defense budget come in nice, simple arithmetic. They're the same kind of talk that led the democracies to neglect their defenses in the 1930s and invited the tragedy of World War II. We must not let that grim chapter of history repeat itself through apathy or neglect.

This is why I'm speaking to you tonight to urge you to tell your senators and congressmen that you know we must continue to restore our military strength. If we stop in midstream, we will send a signal of decline, of lessened will, to friends and adversaries alike. Free people must voluntarily, through open debate and democratic means, meet the challenge that totalitarians pose by compulsion. It's up to us in our time to choose, and choose wisely, between the hard but necessary task of preserving peace and freedom, and the temptation to ignore our duty and blindly hope for the best while the enemies of freedom grow stronger day by day.

The solution is well within our grasp. But to reach it, there is simply no alternative but to continue this year, in this budget, to provide the resources we need to preserve the peace and guarantee our freedom.

Now, thus far tonight I've shared with you my thoughts on the problems of national security we must face together. My predecessors in the Oval Office have appeared before you on other occasions to describe the threat posed by Soviet power and have proposed steps to address that threat. But since the advent of nuclear weapons, those steps have been increasingly directed toward deterrence of aggression through the promise of retaliation.

This approach to stability through offensive threat has worked. We and our allies have succeeded in preventing nuclear war for more than three decades. In recent months, however, my advisers, including in particular the Joint Chiefs of Staff, have underscored the necessity to break out of a future that relies solely on offensive retaliation for our security.

Over the course of these discussions, I've become more and more deeply convinced that the human spirit must be capable of rising above dealing with other nations and human beings by threatening their existence. Feeling this way, I believe we must thoroughly examine every opportunity for reducing tensions and for introducing greater stability into the strategic calculus on both sides.

One of the most important contributions we can make is, of course, to lower the level of all arms, and particularly nuclear arms. We're engaged right now in several negotiations with the Soviet Union to bring about a mutual reduction of weapons. I will report to you a week from tomorrow my thoughts on that score. But let me just say, I'm totally committed to this course.

If the Soviet Union will join with us in our effort to achieve major arms reduction, we will have succeeded in stabilizing the nuclear balance. Nevertheless, it will still be necessary to rely on the specter of retaliation, on mutual threat. And that's a sad commentary on the human condition. Wouldn't it be better to save lives than to avenge them? Are we not capable of demonstrating our peaceful intentions by applying all our abilities and our ingenuity to achieving a truly lasting stability? I think we are. Indeed, we must.

After careful consultation with my advisers, including the Joint Chiefs of Staff, I believe there is a way. Let me share with you a vision of the future which offers hope. It is that we embark on a program to counter the awesome Soviet missile threat with measures that are defensive. Let us turn to the very strengths in technology that spawned our great industrial base and that have given us the quality of life we enjoy today.

What if free people could live secure in the knowledge that their security did not rest upon the threat of instant U.S. retaliation to deter a Soviet attack, that we could intercept and destroy strategic ballistic missiles before they reached our own soil or that of our allies?

I know this is a formidable, technical task, one that may not be accomplished before the end of this century. Yet current technology has attained a level of sophistication where it is reasonable for us to begin this effort. It will take years, probably decades, of effort on many fronts. There will be failures and setbacks, just as there will be successes and breakthroughs. And as we proceed, we must remain constant in preserving the nuclear deterrent and maintaining a solid capability for flexible response. But isn't it worth every investment necessary to free the world from the threat of nuclear war? We know it is.

In the meantime, we will continue to pursue real reductions in nuclear arms, negotiating from a position of strength that can be ensured only by modernizing our strategic forces. At the same time, we must take steps to reduce the risk of a conventional military conflict escalating to nuclear war, by improving our non-nuclear capabilities.

America does possess now the technologies to attain very significant improvements in the effectiveness of our conventional, non-nuclear forces. Proceeding boldly with these new technologies, we can significantly reduce any incentive that the Soviet Union may have to threaten attack against the United States or its allies.

As we pursue our goal of defensive technologies, we recognize that our allies rely upon our strategic offensive power to deter attacks against them. Their vital interests and ours are inextricably linked. Their safety and ours are one. And no change in technology can or will alter that reality. We must and shall continue to honor our commitments.

I clearly recognize that defensive systems have limitations and raise certain problems and ambiguities. If paired with offensive systems, they can be viewed as fostering an aggressive policy, and no one wants that. But with these considerations firmly in mind, I call upon the scientific community in our country, those who gave us nuclear weapons, to turn their great talents now to the cause of mankind and world peace, to give us the means of rendering these nuclear weapons impotent and obsolete.

Tonight, consistent with our obligations of the ABM treaty and recognizing the need for closer consultation with our allies, I'm taking an important first step. I am directing a comprehensive and intensive effort to define a long-term research and development program to begin to achieve our ultimate goal of eliminating the threat posed by strategic nuclear missiles. This could pave the way for arms control measures to eliminate the weapons themselves. We seek neither military superiority nor political advantage. Our only purpose—one all people share—is to search for ways to reduce the danger of nuclear war.

My fellow Americans, tonight we're launching an effort which holds the promise of changing the course of human history. There will be risks, and results take time. But I believe we can do it. As we cross this threshold, I ask for your prayers and your support.

Thank you, good night, and God bless you.

15

ADDRESS ON
CENTRAL AMERICA

In part prompted by the elections in El Salvador where people willing to vote for democracy risked their lives, this speech announced the U.S. plan for stabilizing and providing support to Central America. Reagan said, "Must we just accept the destabilization of an entire region from the Panama Canal to Mexico on our southern border?" He said the U.S. would pursue four key objectives including backing free elections, providing economic assistance, upholding the security of the nations and supporting negotiations between and within the nations. To assist with these efforts, Reagan said he planned to name a special envoy to Central America. In this address, Reagan had to highlight that Central America would not be another Vietnam. He said, "Now, before I go any further, let me say to those who invoke the memory of Vietnam, there is no thought of sending American combat troops to Central America. They are not needed."

Joint Session of Congress

APRIL 27, 1983

———

M r. Speaker, Mr. President, distinguished members of the Congress, honored guests, and my fellow Americans:

A number of times in past years, members of Congress and a president have come together in meetings like this to resolve a crisis. I have asked for this meeting in the hope that we can prevent one.

It would be hard to find many Americans who aren't aware of our stake in the Middle East, the Persian Gulf, or the NATO line dividing the free world from the Communist bloc. And the same could be said for Asia.

But in spite of, or maybe because of, a flurry of stories about places like Nicaragua and El Salvador and, yes, some concerted propaganda, many of us find it hard to believe we have a stake in problems involving those countries. Too many have thought of Central America as just that place way down below Mexico that can't possibly constitute a threat to our well-being. And that's why I've asked for this session. Central America's problems do directly affect the security and the well-being of our own people. And Central America is much closer to the United States than many of the world trouble spots that concern us. So while we work to restore our own economy, we cannot afford to lose sight of our neighbors to the south.

El Salvador is nearer to Texas than Texas is to Massachusetts. Nicaragua is just as close to Miami, San Antonio, San Diego, and Tucson as those cities are to Washington, where we're gathered tonight.

But nearness on the map doesn't even begin to tell the strategic importance of Central America, bordering as it does on the Caribbean—our lifeline to the outside world. Two-thirds of all our foreign trade and petroleum pass through the Panama Canal and the Caribbean. In a European crisis, at least half of our supplies for NATO would go through these areas by sea. It's well to remember that in early 1942, a handful of Hitler's submarines sank more tonnage there than in all of the Atlantic Ocean. And they did this without a single naval base anywhere in the area. And today, the situation is different. Cuba is host to a Soviet combat brigade, a submarine base capable of servicing Soviet submarines, and military air bases visited regularly by Soviet military aircraft.

Because of its importance, the Caribbean Basin is a magnet for adventurism. We're all aware of the Libyan cargo planes refueling in Brazil a few days ago on their way to deliver "medical supplies" to Nicaragua. Brazilian authorities discovered the so-called medical supplies were actually munitions and prevented their delivery.

You may remember that last month, speaking on national television, I showed an aerial photo of an airfield being built on the island of Grenada. Well, if that airfield had been completed, those planes could have refueled there and completed their journey.

If the Nazis during World War II and the Soviets today could recognize the Caribbean and Central America as vital to our interests, shouldn't we, also? For several years now, under two administrations, the United States has been increasing its defense of freedom in the Caribbean Basin. And I can tell you tonight, democracy is beginning to take root in El Salvador, which until a short time ago knew only dictatorship.

The new government is now delivering on its promises of democracy, reforms, and free elections. It wasn't easy, and there was resistance to many of the attempted reforms, with assassinations of some of the reformers. Guerrilla bands and urban terrorists were portrayed in a worldwide propaganda campaign as freedom fighters, representative of the people. Ten days before I came into office, the guerrillas launched what they called a "final offensive" to overthrow the government. And their radio boasted that our new administration would be too late to prevent their victory.

Well, they learned that democracy cannot be so easily defeated. President Carter did not hesitate. He authorized arms and munitions to El Salvador. The guerrilla offensive failed, but not America's will. Every president since this country assumed global responsibilities has known that those responsibilities could only be met if we pursued a bipartisan foreign policy.

As I said a moment ago, the government of El Salvador has been keeping its promises, like the land reform program, which is making thousands of farm tenants farm owners. In a little over three years, twenty percent of the arable land in El Salvador has been redistributed to more than 450,000 people. That's one in ten Salvadorans who have benefited directly from this program.

El Salvador has continued to strive toward an orderly and democratic society. The government promised free elections. On March 28, a little more than a year ago, after months of campaigning by a variety of candidates, the suffering people of El Salvador were offered a chance to vote, to choose the kind of government they wanted. And suddenly, the so-called freedom fighters in the hills were exposed for what they really are—a small minority who want power for themselves and their backers, not democracy for the people. The guerrillas threatened death to anyone who voted. They destroyed hundreds of buses and trucks to keep the people from getting to the polling places. Their slogan was brutal: "Vote today, die tonight." But on election day, an unprecedented eighty percent of the electorate braved ambush and gunfire and trudged for miles, many of them, to vote for freedom. Now, that's truly fighting for freedom. We can never turn our backs on that.

Members of this Congress who went there as observers told me of a woman who was wounded by rifle fire on the way to the polls, who refused to leave the line to have her wound treated until after she had voted. Another woman had been told by the guerrillas that she would be killed when she returned from the polls, and she told the guerrillas, "You can kill me, you can kill my family, you can kill my neighbors. You can't kill us all." The real freedom fighters of El Salvador turned out to be the people of that country—the young, the old, the in-between—more than a million of them out of a population of less than 5 million. The world should respect this courage and not allow it to be belittled or forgotten. And again I say, in good conscience, we can never turn our backs on that.

The democratic political parties and factions in El Salvador are coming together around the common goal of seeking a political solution to their country's problems. New national elections will be held this year, and they will be open to all political parties. The government has invited the guerrillas to participate in the election and is preparing an amnesty law. The people of El Salvador are earning their freedom, and they deserve our moral and material support to protect it.

Yes, there are still major problems regarding human rights, the criminal justice system, and violence against noncombatants. And, like the rest of Central America, El Salvador also faces severe economic problems. But in addition to recession-depressed prices for major agricultural exports, El Salvador's economy is being deliberately sabotaged.

Tonight in El Salvador—because of ruthless guerrilla attacks— much of the fertile land cannot be cultivated; less than half the rolling stock of the railways remains operational; bridges, water facilities, and telephone and electric systems have been destroyed and damaged. In one twenty-two-month period, there were 5,000 interruptions of electrical power. One region was without electricity for a third of the year.

I think Secretary of State Shultz put it very well the other day. "Unable to win the free loyalty of El Salvador's people, the guerrillas," he said, "are deliberately and systematically depriving them of food, water, transportation, light, sanitation, and jobs. And these are the people who claim they want to help the common people."

They don't want elections because they know they'd be defeated. But, as the previous election showed, the Salvadoran people's desire for democracy will not be defeated.

The guerrillas are not embattled peasants, armed with muskets. They're professionals, sometimes with better training and weaponry than the government's soldiers. The Salvadoran battalions that have received U.S. training have been conducting themselves well on the battlefield and with the civilian population. But so far, we've only provided enough money to train one Salvadoran soldier out of ten, fewer than the number of guerrillas that are trained by Nicaragua and Cuba.

And let me set the record straight on Nicaragua, a country next to El Salvador. In 1979 when the new government took over in Nicaragua, after a revolution which overthrew the authoritarian rule of Somoza, everyone hoped for the growth of democracy. We in the United States did, too. By January of 1981, our emergency relief and recovery aid to Nicaragua totaled $118 million—more than provided by any other developed country. In fact, in the first two years of Sandinista rule, the United States directly or indirectly sent five times more aid to Nicaragua than it had in the two years prior to the revolution. Can anyone doubt the generosity and the good faith of the American people?

These were hardly the actions of a nation implacably hostile to Nicaragua. Yet the government of Nicaragua has treated us as an enemy. It has rejected our repeated peace efforts. It has broken its promises to us, to the Organization of American States, and, most important of all, to the people of Nicaragua.

No sooner was victory achieved than a small clique ousted others who had been part of the revolution from having any voice in the government. Humberto Ortega, the minister of defense, declared Marxism-Leninism would be their guide, and so it is.

The government of Nicaragua has imposed a new dictatorship. It has refused to hold the elections it promised. It has seized control of most media and subjects all media to heavy prior censorship. It denied the bishops and priests of the Roman Catholic Church the right to say Mass on radio during Holy Week. It insulted and mocked the pope. It has driven the Miskito Indians from their homelands, burning their villages, destroying their crops, and forcing them into involuntary internment camps far from home. It has moved against the private sector and free labor unions. It condoned mob action against Nicaragua's independent human rights commission and drove the director of that commission into exile.

In short, after all these acts of repression by the government, is it any wonder that opposition has formed? Contrary to propaganda, the opponents of the Sandinistas are not diehard supporters of the previous Somoza regime. In fact, many are anti-Somoza heroes and fought beside the Sandinistas to bring down the Somoza government. Now they've been denied any part in the new government because they truly wanted democracy for Nicaragua and they still do. Others are Miskito Indians fighting for their homes, their lands, and their lives.

The Sandinista revolution in Nicaragua turned out to be just an exchange of one set of autocratic rules for another, and the people still have no freedom, no democratic rights, and more poverty. Even worse than its predecessor, it is helping Cuba and the Soviets to destabilize our hemisphere.

Meanwhile, the government of El Salvador, making every effort to guarantee democracy, free labor unions, freedom of religion, and a free press, is under attack by guerrillas dedicated to the same philosophy that prevails in Nicaragua, Cuba, and, yes, the Soviet Union. Violence has been Nicaragua's most important export to the world. It is the ultimate in hypocrisy for the unelected Nicaraguan government to charge that we seek their overthrow, when they're doing everything they can to bring down the elected government of El Salvador. [Applause] Thank You. The guerrilla attacks are directed from a headquarters in Managua, the capital of Nicaragua.

But let us be clear as to the American attitude toward the government of Nicaragua. We do not seek its overthrow. Our interest is to ensure that it does not infect its neighbors through the export of subversion and violence. Our purpose, in conformity with American and international law, is to prevent the flow of arms to El Salvador, Honduras, Guatemala and Costa Rica. We have attempted to have a dialogue with the government of Nicaragua, but it persists in its efforts to spread violence.

We should not, and we will not, protect the Nicaraguan government from the anger of its own people. But we should, through diplomacy, offer an alternative. And as Nicaragua ponders its options, we can and will—with all the resources of diplomacy—protect each country of Central America from the danger of war.

Even Costa Rica, Central America's oldest and strongest democracy—a government so peaceful it doesn't even have an army—is the object of bullying and threats from Nicaragua's dictators.

Nicaragua's neighbors know that Sandinista promises of peace, nonalliance, and nonintervention have not been kept. Some thirty-six new military bases have been built; there were only thirteen during the Somoza years. Nicaragua's new army numbers 25,000 men, supported by a militia of 50,000. It is the largest army in Central America, supplemented by 2,000 Cuban military and security advisers. It is equipped with the most modern weapons—dozens of Soviet-made tanks, 800 Soviet-bloc trucks, Soviet 152 mm howitzers, 100 anti-aircraft guns, plus planes and helicopters. There are additional thousands of civilian advisers from Cuba, the Soviet Union, East Germany, Libya, and the PLO. And we're attacked because we have fifty-five military trainers in El Salvador.

The goal of the professional guerrilla movements in Central America is as simple as it is sinister: to destabilize the entire region from the Panama Canal to Mexico. And if you doubt beyond this point, just consider what Cayetano Carpio, the now-deceased

Salvadoran guerrilla leader, said earlier this month. Carpio said that after El Salvador falls, El Salvador and Nicaragua would be "arm-in-arm and struggling for the total liberation of Central America."

Nicaragua's dictatorial junta, who themselves made war and won power operating from bases in Honduras and Costa Rica, like to pretend that they are today being attacked by forces based in Honduras. The fact is, it is Nicaragua's government that threatens Honduras, not the reverse. It is Nicaragua who has moved heavy tanks close to the border, and Nicaragua who speaks of war. It was Nicaraguan radio that announced on April 8 the creation of a new, unified, revolutionary coordinating board to push forward the Marxist struggle in Honduras.

Nicaragua, supported by weapons and military resources provided by the Communist bloc, represses its own people, refuses to make peace, and sponsors a guerrilla war against El Salvador.

President Truman's words are as apt today as they were in 1947 when he, too, spoke before a joint session of the Congress:

"At the present moment in world history, nearly every nation must choose between alternate ways of life. The choice is not too often a free one. One way of life is based upon the will of the majority and is distinguished by free institutions, representative government, free elections, guarantees of individual liberty, freedom of speech and religion, and freedom from political oppression. The second way of life is based upon the will of a minority forcibly imposed upon the majority. It relies upon terror and oppression, a controlled press and radio, fixed elections, and the suppression of personal freedoms.

"I believe that it must be the policy of the United States to support free peoples who are resisting attempted subjugation by armed minorities or by outside pressures. I believe that we must assist free peoples to work out their own destinies in their own way. I believe that our help should be primarily through economic and financial aid, which is essential to economic stability and orderly political processes.

"Collapse of free institutions and loss of independence would be disastrous not only for them but for the world. Discouragement and possibly failure would quickly be the lot of neighboring peoples striving to maintain their freedom and independence."

The countries of Central America are smaller than the nations that prompted President Truman's message. But the political and strategic stakes are the same. Will our response—economic, social, military—be as appropriate and successful as Mr. Truman's bold solutions to the problems of postwar Europe?

Some people have forgotten the successes of those years and the decades of peace, prosperity, and freedom they secured. Some people talk as though the United States were incapable of acting effectively in international affairs without risking war or damaging those we seek to help.

Are democracies required to remain passive while threats to their security and prosperity accumulate? Must we just accept the destabilization of an entire region from the Panama Canal to Mexico on our southern border? Must we sit by while independent nations of this hemisphere are integrated into the most aggressive empire the modern world has seen? Must we wait while Central Americans are driven from their homes like the more than a million who have sought refuge out of Afghanistan, or the 1-plus million who have fled Indochina, or the more than a million Cubans who have fled Castro's Caribbean Utopia? Must we, by default, leave the people of El Salvador no choice but to flee their homes, creating another tragic human exodus?

I don't believe there's a majority in the Congress or the country that counsels passivity, resignation, defeatism, in the face of this challenge to freedom and security in our own hemisphere. [Applause] Thank you. Thank you.

I do not believe that a majority of the Congress or the country is prepared to stand by passively while the people of Central America are delivered to totalitarianism and we ourselves are left vulnerable to new dangers.

Only last week, an official of the Soviet Union reiterated Brezhnev's threat to station nuclear missiles in this hemisphere, five minutes from the United States. Like an echo, Nicaragua's Commandante Daniel Ortega confirmed that, if asked, his country would consider accepting those missiles. I understand that today they may be having second thoughts.

Now, before I go any further, let me say to those who invoke the memory of Vietnam, there is no thought of sending American combat troops to Central America. They are not needed.

Thank you. And, as I say, they are not needed and, indeed, they have not been requested there. All our neighbors ask of us is assistance in training and arms to protect themselves while they build a better, freer life.

We must continue to encourage peace among the nations of Central America. We must support the regional efforts now under way to promote solutions to regional problems.

We cannot be certain that the Marxist-Leninist bands who believe war is an instrument of politics will be readily discouraged. It's crucial that we do not become discouraged before they do. Otherwise, the region's freedom will be lost and our security damaged in ways that can hardly be calculated

If Central America were to fall, what would the consequences be for our position in Asia, Europe, and for alliances such as NATO? If the United States cannot respond to a threat near our own borders, why should Europeans or Asians believe that we're seriously concerned about threats to them? If the Soviets can assume that nothing short of an actual attack on the United States will provoke an American response, which ally, which friend will trust us then?

The Congress shares both the power and the responsibility for our foreign policy. Tonight, I ask you, the Congress, to join me in a bold, generous approach to the problems of peace and poverty, democracy and dictatorship in the region. Join me in a program that prevents Communist victory in the short run, but goes beyond, to produce for the deprived people of the area the reality of present progress and the promise of more to come.

Let us lay the foundation for a bipartisan approach to sustain the independence and freedom of the countries of Central America. We in the administration reach out to you in this spirit.

We will pursue four basic goals in Central America:

First, in response to decades of inequity and indifference, we will support democracy, reform, and human freedom. This means using our assistance, our powers of persuasion, and our legitimate leverage to bolster humane democratic systems where they already exist and to help countries on their way to that goal complete the process as quickly as human institutions can be changed. Elections in El Salvador and also in Nicaragua must be open to all, fair and safe. The international community must help. We will work at human rights problems, not walk away from them.

Second, in response to the challenge of world recession and, in the case of El Salvador, to the unrelenting campaign of economic sabotage by the guerrillas, we will support economic development. And by a margin of two to one our aid is economic now, not military. Seventy-seven cents out of every dollar we will spend in the area this year goes for food, fertilizers, and other essentials for economic growth and development. And our economic program goes beyond traditional aid. The Caribbean Initiative introduced in the House earlier today will provide powerful trade and investment incentives to help these countries achieve self-sustaining economic growth without exporting U.S. jobs. Our goal must be to focus our immense and growing technology to enhance healthcare, agriculture, industry, and to ensure that we who inhabit this interdependent region come to know and understand each other better, retaining our diverse identities, respecting our diverse traditions and institutions.

And, third, in response to the military challenge from Cuba and Nicaragua—to their deliberate use of force to spread tyranny—we will support the security of the region's threatened nations. We do not view security assistance as an end in itself, but as a shield for democratization, economic development, and diplomacy. No amount of reform will bring peace so long as guerrillas believe they will win by force. No amount of economic help will suffice if guerrilla units can destroy roads and bridges and power stations and crops, again and again, with impunity. But with better training and material help, our neighbors can hold off the guerrillas and give democratic reform time to take root.

And, fourth, we will support dialog and negotiations both among the countries of the region and within each country. The terms and conditions of participation in elections are negotiable. Costa Rica is a shining example of democracy. Honduras has made the move from military rule to democratic government. Guatemala is pledged to the same course. The United States will work toward a political solution in Central America which will serve the interests of the democratic process.

To support these diplomatic goals, I offer these assurances: The United States will support any agreement among Central American countries for the withdrawal, under fully verifiable and reciprocal conditions, of all foreign military and security advisers and troops. We want to help opposition groups join the political process in all countries and complete by ballots instead of bullets. We will support any verifiable, reciprocal agreement among Central American countries on the renunciation of support for insurgencies on neighbors' territory. And, finally, we desire to help Central America end its costly arms race and will support any verifiable, reciprocal agreements on the nonimportation of offensive weapons.

To move us toward these goals more rapidly, I am tonight announcing my intention to name an ambassador-at-large as my special envoy to Central America. He or she will report to me through the secretary of state. The ambassador's responsibilities will be to lend U.S. support to the efforts of regional governments to bring peace to this troubled area and to work closely with the

Congress to assure the fullest possible, bipartisan coordination of our policies toward the region.

What I'm asking for is prompt congressional approval for the full reprogramming of funds for key current economic and security programs so that the people of Central America can hold the line against externally supported aggression. In addition, I am asking for prompt action on the supplemental request in these same areas to carry us through the current fiscal year and for early and favorable congressional action on my requests for fiscal year 1984.

And finally, I am asking that the bipartisan consensus, which last year acted on the trade and tax provisions of the Caribbean Basin Initiative in the House, again take the lead to move this vital proposal to the floor of both chambers. And, as I said before, the greatest share of these requests is targeted toward economic and humanitarian aid, not military.

What the administration is asking for on behalf of freedom in Central America is so small, so minimal, considering what is at stake. The total amount requested for aid to all of Central America in 1984 is about $600 million. That's less than one-tenth of what Americans will spend this year on coin-operated video games.

In summation, I say to you that tonight there can be no question: The national security of all the Americas is at stake in Central America. If we cannot defend ourselves there, we cannot expect to prevail elsewhere. Our credibility would collapse, our alliances would crumble, and the safety of our homeland would be put in jeopardy.

We have a vital interest, a moral duty, and a solemn responsibility. This is not a partisan issue. It is a question of our meeting our moral responsibility to ourselves, our friends, and our posterity. It is a duty that falls on all of us—the president, the Congress, and the people. We must perform it together. Who among us would wish to bear responsibility for failing to meet our shared obligation?

Thank you, God bless you, and good night.

16

Soviet Attack on KAL Flight 007

This flight from New York was headed to Seoul, South Korea with 269 passengers and crew on board. After refueling in Alaska, the plane somehow ended up in Russian air space and was shot down by a Russian fighter pilot. Among the passengers was Rep. Larry McDonald of Georgia. Reaction in the U.S. and elsewhere was swift with Reagan describing the incident as "an act of barbarism, both of a society which wantonly disregards individual rights and the value of human life, and seeks constantly to expand and dominate other nations."

Visibly distressed, Reagan played an audiotape of the pilots speaking in Russian, supporting his view that they had responded to orders to shoot down what was clearly visible as a civilian plane. The President said he would ask Congress to pass a joint resolution condemning the Soviet crime and he also called for an emergency meeting of the UN Security Council.

Address to the Nation

SEPTEMBER 5, 1983

––––––

M y fellow Americans:
I'm coming before you tonight about the Korean airline massacre, the attack by the Soviet Union against 269 innocent men, women, and children aboard an unarmed Korean passenger plane. This crime against humanity must never be forgotten, here or throughout the world.

Our prayers tonight are with the victims and their families in their time of terrible grief. Our hearts go out to them—to brave people like Kathryn McDonald, the wife of a congressman, whose composure and eloquence on the day of her husband's death moved us all. He will be sorely missed by all of us here in government. The parents of one slain couple wired me: "Our daughter—and her husband—died on Korean Airlines Flight 007. Their deaths were the result of the Soviet Union violating every concept of human rights." The emotions of these parents—grief, shock, anger—are shared by civilized people everywhere. From around the world press accounts reflect an explosion of condemnation by people everywhere.

Let me state as plainly as I can: There was absolutely no justification, either legal or moral, for what the Soviets did. One newspaper in India said, "If every passenger plane is fair game for home air forces it will be the end to civil aviation as we know it."

This is not the first time the Soviet Union has shot at and hit a civilian airliner when it overflew its territory. In another tragic incident in 1978, the Soviets so shot down an unarmed civilian airliner after having positively identified it as such. In that instance, the Soviet interceptor pilot clearly identified the civilian markings on the side of the aircraft, repeatedly questioned the order to fire on a civilian airliner, and was ordered to shoot it down anyway. The aircraft was hit with a missile and made a crash landing. Several innocent people lost their lives in this attack, killed by shrapnel from the blast of a Soviet missile.

Is this a practice of other countries in the world? The answer is no. Commercial aircraft from the Soviet Union and Cuba on a number of occasions have overflown sensitive United States military facilities. They weren't shot down. We and other civilized countries believe in the tradition of offering help to mariners and pilots who are lost or in distress on the sea or in the air. We believe in following procedures to prevent a tragedy, not to provoke one.

But despite the savagery of their crime, the universal reaction against it, and the evidence of their complicity, the Soviets still refuse to tell the truth. They have persistently refused to admit that their pilot fired on the Korean aircraft. Indeed, they've not even told their own people that a plane was shot down. They have spun a confused tale of tracking the plane by radar until it just mysteriously disappeared from their radar screens, that no one fired a shot of any kind. But then they coupled this with charges that it was a spy plane sent by us and that their planes fired tracer bullets past the plane as a warning that it was in Soviet airspace.

Let me recap for a moment and present the incontrovertible evidence that we have. The Korean airliner, a Boeing 747, left Anchorage, Alaska, bound for Seoul, Korea, on a course south and west which would take it across Japan. Out over the Pacific, in international waters, it was for a brief time in the vicinity of one of our reconnaissance planes, an RC-135, on a routine mission. At no time was the RC-135 in Soviet airspace. The Korean airliner flew on, and the two planes were soon widely separated.

The 747 is equipped with the most modern computerized navigation facilities, but a computer must respond to input provided by human hands. No one will ever know whether a mistake was made in giving the computer the course or whether there was a malfunction. Whichever, the 747 was flying a course further to the west than it was supposed to fly—a course which took it into Soviet airspace. The Soviets tracked this plane for two and a half hours while it flew a straight-line course at 30–35,000 feet. Only civilian airliners fly in such a manner. At one point, the Korean pilot gave Japanese air control his position as east of Hokkaido, Japan, showing that he was unaware they were off course by as much as or more than a hundred miles.

The Soviets scrambled jet interceptors from a base on Sakhalin Island. Japanese ground sites recorded the interceptor planes' radio transmissions—their conversations with their own ground control. We only have the voices from the pilots; the Soviet ground-to-air transmissions were not recorded. It's plain, however, from the pilot's words that he's responding to orders and queries from his own ground control. Here is a brief segment of the tape which we're going to play in its entirety for the United Nations Security Council tomorrow. [At this point, an audiotape of Soviet military pilots speaking in Russian was played for twenty-two seconds.]

Those were the voices of the Soviet pilots. In this tape, the pilot who fired the missile describes his search for what he calls the target. He reports he has it in sight; indeed, he pulls up to within about a mile of the Korean plane, mentions its flashing strobe light and that its navigation lights are on. He then reports he's reducing speed to get behind the airliner, gives his distance from the plane at various points in this maneuver, and finally announces what can only be called the Korean airline massacre. He says he has locked on the radar, which aims his missiles, has launched those missiles, the target has been destroyed, and he is breaking off the attack.

Let me point out something here having to do with his close-up view of the airliner on what we know was a clear night with a half moon. The 747 has a unique and distinctive silhouette, unlike any other plane in the world. There is no way a pilot could mistake this for anything other than a civilian airliner. And if that isn't enough, let me point out our RC-135 that I mentioned earlier had been back at its base in Alaska, on the ground for an hour, when the murderous attack took place over the Sea of Japan.

And make no mistake about it, this attack was not just against ourselves or the Republic of Korea. This was the Soviet Union against the world and the moral precepts which guide human relations among people everywhere. It was an act of barbarism, born of a society which wantonly disregards individual rights and the value of human life, and seeks constantly to expand and dominate other nations. They deny the deed, but in their conflicting and misleading protestations, the Soviets reveal that, yes, shooting down a plane—even one with hundreds of innocent men, women, children, and babies—is a part of their normal procedure if that plane is in what they claim as their airspace.

They owe the world an apology and an offer to join the rest of the world in working out a system to protect against this ever happening again. Among the rest of us there is one protective measure: an international radio wavelength on which pilots can communicate with planes of other nations if they are in trouble or lost. Soviet military planes are not so equipped, because that would make it easier for pilots who might want to defect.

Our request to send vessels into Soviet waters to search for wreckage and bodies has received no satisfactory answer. Bereaved families of the Japanese victims were harassed by Soviet patrol boats when they tried to get near where the plane is believed to have gone down, in order to hold a ceremony for their dead. But we shouldn't be surprised by such inhuman brutality. Memories come back of Czechoslovakia, Hungary, Poland, the gassing of villages in Afghanistan. If the massacre and their subsequent conduct is intended to intimidate, they have failed in their purpose. From every corner of the globe the word is defiance in the face of this unspeakable act, and defiance of the system which excuses it and tries to cover it up. With our horror and our sorrow, there is a righteous and terrible anger. It would be easy to think in terms of vengeance, but that is not a proper answer. We want justice and action, to see that this never happens again.

Our immediate challenge to this atrocity is to ensure that we make the skies safer and that we seek just compensation for the families of those who were killed. Since my return to Washington, we've held long meetings, the most recent yesterday with the congressional leadership. There was a feeling of unity in the room, and I received a number of constructive suggestions. We will continue to work with the Congress regarding our response to this massacre. As you know, we immediately made known to the world the shocking facts as honestly and completely as they came to us.

We have notified the Soviets that we will not renew our bilateral agreement for cooperation in the field of transportation so long as they threaten the security of civil aviation. Since 1981 the Soviet airline Aeroflot has been denied the right to fly to the United States. We have reaffirmed that order and are examining additional steps we can take with regard to Aeroflot facilities in this country. We're cooperating with other countries to find better means to ensure the safety of civil aviation and to join us in not accepting Aeroflot as a normal member of the international civil air community unless and until the Soviets satisfy the cries of humanity for justice. I am pleased to report that Canada today suspended Aeroflot's landing and refueling privileges for sixty days.

We have joined with other countries to press the International Civil Aviation Organization to investigate this crime at an urgent special session of the Council. At the same time, we're listening most carefully to private groups, both American and international, airline pilots, passenger associations, and others, who have a special interest in civil air safety. I am asking the Congress to pass a joint resolution of condemnation of this Soviet crime. We have informed the Soviets that we're suspending negotiations on several bilateral arrangements we had under consideration.

Along with Korea and Japan, we called an emergency meeting of the UN Security Council, which began on Friday. On that first day, Korea, Japan, Canada, Australia, the Netherlands, Pakistan, France, China, the United Kingdom, Zaire, New Zealand, and West Germany all joined us in denouncing the Soviet action and expressing our horror. We expect to hear from additional countries as debate resumes tomorrow.

We intend to work with the thirteen countries who had citizens aboard the Korean airliner to seek reparations for the families of all those who were killed. The United States will be making a claim against the Soviet Union within the next week to obtain compensation for the benefit of the victims' survivors. Such compensation is an absolute moral duty which the Soviets must assume. In the economic area in general, we're redoubling our efforts with our allies to end the flow of military and strategic items to the Soviet Union.

Secretary Shultz is going to Madrid to meet with representatives of thirty-five countries who, for three years, have been negotiating an agreement having to do with, among other things, human rights. Foreign Minister Gromyko of the Soviet Union is scheduled to attend that meeting. If he does come to the meeting, Secretary Shultz is going to present him with our demands for disclosure of the facts, corrective action, and concrete assurances that such a thing will not happen again and that restitution be made.

As we work with other countries to see that justice is done, the real test of our resolve is whether we have the will to remain strong, steady, and united. I believe more than ever—as evidenced by your thousands and thousands of wires and phone calls in these last few days—that we do. I have outlined some of the steps we're taking in response to the tragic massacre. There's something I've always believed in, which now seems more important than ever. The Congress will be facing key national security issues when it returns from recess. There has been legitimate difference of opinion on this subject, I know, but I urge the members of that distinguished body to ponder long and hard the Soviets' aggression as they consider the security and safety of our people—indeed, all people who believe in freedom.

Senator Henry Jackson, a wise and revered statesman and one who probably understood the Soviets as well as any American in history, warned us, "the greatest threat the United States now faces is posed by the Soviet Union." But Senator Jackson said, "If America maintains a strong deterrent—and only if it does—this nation will continue to be a leader in the crucial quest for enduring peace among nations. The late senator made those statements in July on the Senate floor, speaking in behalf of the MX missile program he considered vital to restore America's strategic parity with the Soviets.

When John F. Kennedy was president, defense spending as a share of the federal budget was seventy percent greater than it is today. Since then, the Soviet Union has carried on the most massive military buildup the world has ever seen. Until they're willing to join the rest of the world community, we must maintain the strength to deter their aggression.

But while we do so, we must not give up our effort to bring them into the world community of nations. Peace through strength as long as necessary, but never giving up our effort to bring peace closer through mutual, verifiable reduction in the weapons of war. I've told you of negotiations we've suspended as a result of the Korean airline massacre; but we cannot, we must not, give up our effort to reduce the arsenals of destructive weapons threatening the world. Ambassador Nitze has returned to Geneva to resume the negotiations on intermediate-range nuclear weapons in Europe. Equally, we will continue to press for arms reductions in the START talks that resume in October. We are more determined than ever to reduce and, if possible, eliminate the threat hanging over mankind.

We know it will be hard to make a nation that rules its own people through force to cease using force against the rest of the world. But we must try. This is not a role we sought. We preach no manifest destiny. But like Americans who began this country and brought forth this last, best hope of mankind, history has asked much of the Americans of our own time. Much we have already given; much more we must be prepared to give.

Let us have faith, in Abraham Lincoln's words, "that right makes might, and in that faith let us, to the end, dare to do our duty as we understand it." If we do, if we stand together and move forward with courage, then history will record that some good did come from this monstrous wrong that we will carry with us and remember for the rest of our lives.

Thank you. God bless you, and good night.

17

COMMEMORATING THE 40th ANNIVERSARY OF D-DAY

In this emotional speech, the President cited the recollections of Lisa Zanatta Henn, speaking of her father Private Zanatta's experiences in World War II. Perhaps in a reference to the Russian intention to continue to invade countries, Reagan talked of the Allied forces reaching the Normandy beaches as liberators, not conquerors. Praising the French Resistance as well as other troops, Reagan went on to say, "We celebrate the triumph of democracy. We reaffirm the unity of democratic people who fought a war and then joined with the vanquished in a firm resolve to keep the peace." Again mentioning the relationship between the U.S. and its present day allies, Reagan continued, "From a terrible war we learned that unity made us invincible; now, in peace, that same unity makes us secure. Our alliance, forged in the crucible of war, tempered and shaped by the realities of the post-war world, has succeeded."

Omaha Beach Memorial, Normandy, France

JUNE 6, 1984

———

We stand today at a place of battle, one that forty years ago saw and felt the worst of war. Men bled and died here for a few feet of—or inches of—sand, as bullets and shell-fire cut through their ranks. About them, General Omar Bradley later said, "Every man who set foot on Omaha Beach that day was a hero."

Some who survived the battle of June 6, 1944, are here today. Others who hoped to return never did.

"Someday, Lis, I'll go back," said Private First Class Peter Robert Zanatta, of the Thirty-seventh Engineer Combat Battalion and first assault wave to hit Omaha Beach. "I'll go back and I'll see it all again. I'll see the beach, the barricades, and the graves."

Those words of Private Zanatta come to us from his daughter, Lisa Zanatta Henn, in a heart-rending story about the event her father spoke of so often. "In his words, the Normandy invasion would change his life forever," she said. She tells some of his stories of World War II but says of her father, "the story to end all stories was D-Day."

"He made me feel the fear of being on the boat waiting to land. I can smell the ocean and feel the sea sickness. I can see the looks on his fellow soldiers' faces—the fear, the anguish, the uncertainty of what lay ahead. And when they landed, I can feel the strength and courage of the men who took those first steps through the tide to what must have surely looked like instant death."

Private Zanatta's daughter wrote to me: "I don't know how or why I can feel this emptiness, this fear, or this determination, but I do. Maybe it's the bond I had with my father. All I know is that it brings tears to my eyes to think about my father as a twenty-year-old boy having to face that beach."

The anniversary of D-Day was always special to her family. And like all the families of those who went to war, she describes how she came to realize her own father's survival was a miracle: "So many men died. I know that my father watched many of his friends be killed. I know that he must have died inside a little each time. But his explanation to me was, 'You did what you had to do, and you kept on going.'"

When men like Private Zanatta and all our Allied forces stormed the beaches of Normandy forty years ago they came not as conquerors, but as liberators. When these troops swept across the French countryside and into the forests of Belgium and Luxembourg they came not to take, but to return what had been wrongfully seized. When our forces marched into Germany they came not to prey on a brave and defeated people, but to nurture the seeds of democracy among those who yearned to be free again.

We salute them today. But, Mr. President [Francois Mitterand of France], we also salute those who, like yourself, were already engaging the enemy inside your beloved country—the French Resistance. Your valiant struggle for France did so much to cripple the enemy and spur the advance of the armies of liberation. The French Forces of the Interior will forever personify courage and national spirit. They will be a timeless inspiration to all who are free and to all who would be free.

Today, in their memory, and for all who fought here, we celebrate the triumph of democracy. We reaffirm the unity of democratic people who fought a war and then joined with the vanquished in a firm resolve to keep the peace.

From a terrible war we learned that unity made us invincible; now, in peace, that same unity makes us secure. We sought to bring all freedom-loving nations together in a community dedicated to the defense and preservation of our sacred values. Our alliance, forged in the crucible of war, tempered and shaped by the realities of the post-war world, has succeeded. In Europe, the threat has been contained, the peace has been kept.

Today, the living here assembled—officials, veterans, citizens—are a tribute to what was achieved here forty years ago. This land is secure. We are free. These things are worth fighting and dying for.

Lisa Zanatta Henn began her story by quoting her father, who promised that he would return to Normandy. She ended with a promise to her father, who died eight years ago of cancer: "I'm going there, Dad, and I'll see the beaches and the barricades and the monuments. I'll see the graves, and I'll put flowers there just like you wanted to do. I'll never forget what you went through, Dad, nor will I let anyone else forget. And, Dad, I'll always be proud."

Through the words of his loving daughter, who is here with us today, a D-Day veteran has shown us the meaning of this day far better than any president can. It is enough to say about Private Zanatta and all the men of honor and courage who fought beside him four decades ago: We will always remember. We will always be proud. We will always be prepared, so we may always be free. Thank you.

18

THE BOYS OF
POINTE DU HOC

Heralded by many as one of Reagan's most powerful speeches, this oration is essentially an homage to all soldiers. Reagan focuses on one of the most significant battles of World War II when a single company of elite Army rangers scaled a 100 foot cliff to launch an assault on a German arsenal of guns. The weapons were not there but the German gunners ended up killing half the U.S. soldiers. Speaking before some 60 veterans and world leaders including Queen Elizabeth II, Queen Beatrix of the Netherlands, and Prime Minister Trudeau of Canada, Reagan's speech was occasionally halted as emotions overwhelmed him. He spoke directly to some of the soldiers who had fought at this site, noting, "These are the men who took the cliffs. These are the champions who helped free a continent. These are the heroes who helped end a war."

U.S. Ranger Monument at Pointe du Hoc, Normandy, France

JUNE 6, 1984

W e're here to mark that day in history when the Allied peoples joined in battle to reclaim this continent for liberty. For four long years, much of Europe had been under a terrible shadow. Free nations had fallen, Jews cried out in the camps, millions cried out for liberation. Europe was enslaved, and the world prayed for its rescue. Here in Normandy the rescue began. Here the Allies stood and fought against tyranny in a giant undertaking unparalleled in human history.

We stand on a lonely, windswept point on the northern shore of France. The air is soft, but forty years ago at this moment, the air was dense with smoke and the cries of men, and the air was filled with the crack of rifle fire and the roar of cannon. At dawn, on the morning of the sixth of June 1944, 225 Rangers jumped off the British landing craft and ran to the bottom of these cliffs. Their mission was one of the most difficult and daring of the invasion: to climb these sheer and desolate cliffs and take out the enemy guns. The Allies had been told that some of the mightiest of these guns were here and they would be trained on the beaches to stop the Allied advance.

The Rangers looked up and saw the enemy soldiers—at the edge of the cliffs, shooting down at them with machine guns and throwing grenades. And the American Rangers began to climb. They shot rope ladders over the face of these cliffs and began to pull themselves up. When one Ranger fell, another would take his place. When one rope was cut, a Ranger would grab another and begin his climb again. They climbed, shot back, and held their footing. Soon, one by one, the Rangers pulled themselves over the top, and in seizing the firm land at the top of these cliffs, they began to seize back the continent of Europe. Two hundred twenty-five came here. After two days of fighting only 90 could still bear arms.

Behind me is a memorial that symbolizes the Ranger daggers that were thrust into the top of these cliffs. And before me are the men who put them there.

These are the boys of Pointe du Hoc. These are the men who took the cliffs. These are the champions who helped free a continent. These are the heroes who helped end a war.

Gentlemen, I look at you and I think of the words of Stephen Spender's poem. You are men who in your lives "fought for life and left the vivid air signed with your honor."

Forty summers have passed since the battle that you fought here. You were young the day you took these cliffs; some of you were hardly more than boys, with the deepest joys of life before you. Yet you risked everything here. Why? Why did you do it? What impelled you to put aside the instinct for self-preservation and risk your lives to take these cliffs? What inspired all the men of the armies that met here? We look at you and somehow we know the answer. It was faith and belief; it was loyalty and love.

The men of Normandy had faith that what they were doing was right, faith that they fought for all humanity, faith that a just God would grant them mercy on this beachhead or on the next. It was the deep knowledge—and pray God we have not lost it—that there is a profound moral difference between the use of force for liberation and the use of force for conquest. You were here to liberate, not to conquer, and so you and those others did not doubt your cause. And you were right not to doubt.

You all knew that some things are worth dying for. One's country is worth dying for, and democracy is worth dying for, because it's the most deeply honorable form of government ever devised by man. All of you loved liberty. All of you were willing to fight tyranny, and you knew the people of your countries were behind you.

19
WITH HEART AND HAND

President Reagan covered both domestic problems including the economy as well as the position of the country in relation to the rest of the world. And, as he did in his first Inaugural Address, he spoke about freedom and its importance in preserving peace and conquering poverty.

Against the backdrop of a robust American economy, Reagan called for a simplification of the tax code to lower rates and make the system more equitable. He said it was time to reduce the national debt and called for a balanced budget. To reach that goal, he was requesting a freeze on government spending for the coming year.

Of course, Reagan was not willing to forgo a mention of the Soviet Union and he again said he hoped to make an agreement with the Soviets to rid the world of the threat of nuclear weapons.

Second Inaugural Address

JANUARY 21, 1985

S enator Mathias, Chief Justice Burger, Vice President Bush, Speaker O'Neill, Senator Dole, Reverend Clergy, members of my family and friends, and my fellow citizens:

This day has been made brighter with the presence here of one who, for a time, has been absent—Senator John Stennis.

God bless you, and welcome back.

There is, however, one who is not with us today: Representative Gillis Long of Louisiana left us last night. I wonder if we could all join in a moment of silent prayer. [Moment of silent prayer.] Amen.

There are no words adequate to express my thanks for the great honor that you have bestowed on me. I will do my utmost to be deserving of your trust.

This is, as Senator Mathias told us, the fiftieth time that we the people have celebrated this historic occasion. When the first president, George Washington, placed his hand upon the Bible, he stood less than a single day's journey by horseback from raw, untamed wilderness. There were 4 million Americans in a union of thirteen states. Today we are sixty times as many in a union of fifty states. We have lighted the world with our inventions, gone to the aid of mankind wherever in the world there was a cry for help, journeyed to the moon and safely returned. So much has changed. And yet we stand together as we did two centuries ago.

When I took this oath four years ago, I did so in a time of economic stress. Voices were raised saying we had to look to our past for the greatness and glory. But we, the present-day Americans, are not given to looking backward. In this blessed land, there is always a better tomorrow.

Four years ago, I spoke to you of a new beginning and we have accomplished that. But in another sense, our new beginning is a continuation of that beginning created two centuries ago when, for the first time in history, government, the people said, is not our master, it is our servant; its only power that which we the people allow it to have.

That system has never failed us; but, for a time, we failed the system. We asked things of government that government was not equipped to give. We yielded authority to the national government that properly belonged to states or to local governments or to the people themselves. We allowed taxes and inflation to rob us of our earnings and savings and watched the great industrial machine that had made us the most productive people on earth slow down and the number of unemployed increase.

By 1980, we knew it was time to renew our faith, to strive with all our strength toward the ultimate in individual freedom consistent with an orderly society.

We believed then and now there are no limits to growth and human progress when men and women are free to follow their dreams.

And we were right to believe that. Tax rates have been reduced, inflation cut dramatically, and more people are employed than ever before in our history.

We are creating a nation once again vibrant, robust, and alive. But there are many mountains yet to climb. We will not rest until every American enjoys the fullness of freedom, dignity, and opportunity as our birthright. It is our birthright as citizens of this great republic, and we'll meet this challenge.

These will be years when Americans have restored their confidence and tradition of progress; when our values of faith, family, work, and neighborhood were restated for a modern age; when our economy was finally freed from government's grip; when we made sincere efforts at meaningful arms reduction, rebuilding our defenses, our economy, and developing new technologies, and helped preserve peace in a troubled world; when Americans courageously supported the struggle for liberty, self-government, and free enterprise throughout the world and turned the tide of history away from totalitarian darkness and into the warm sunlight of human freedom.

My fellow citizens, our nation is poised for greatness. We must do what we know is right and do it with all our might. Let history say of us, "These were golden years—when the American Revolution was reborn, when freedom gained new life, when America reached for her best."

Our two-party system has served us well over the years, but never better than in those times of great challenge when we came together not as Democrats or Republicans, but as Americans united in a common cause.

Two of our Founding Fathers, a Boston lawyer named Adams and a Virginia planter named Jefferson, members of that remarkable group who met in Independence Hall and dared to think they could start the world over again, left us an important lesson. They had become political rivals in the presidential election of 1800. Then years later, when both were retired and age had softened their anger, they began to speak to each other again through letters. A bond was reestablished between those two who had helped create this government of ours.

In 1826, the fiftieth anniversary of the Declaration of Independence, they both died. They died on the same day, within a few hours of each other, and that day was the Fourth of July.

In one of those letters exchanged in the sunset of their lives, Jefferson wrote: "It carries me back to the times when, beset with difficulties and dangers, we were fellow laborers in the same cause, struggling for what is most valuable to man, his right to self-government. Laboring always at the same oar, with some wave ever ahead threatening to overwhelm us, and yet passing harmless, we rode through the storm with heart and hand."

Well, with heart and hand, let us stand as one today: One people under God determined that our future shall be worthy of our past. As we do, we must not repeat the well-intentioned errors of our past. We must never again abuse the trust of working men and women, by sending their earnings on a futile chase after the spiraling demands of a bloated federal establishment. You elected us in 1980 to end this prescription for disaster, and I don't believe you re-elected us in 1984 to reverse course.

At the heart of our efforts is one idea vindicated by twenty-five straight months of economic growth: Freedom and incentives unleash the drive and entrepreneurial genius that are the core of human progress.

We have begun to increase the rewards for work, savings, and investment; reduce the increase in the cost and size of government and its interference in people's lives.

We must simplify our tax system, make it more fair, and bring the rates down for all who work and earn. We must think anew and move with a new boldness, so every American who seeks work can find work; so the least among us shall have an equal chance to achieve the greatest things—to be heroes who heal our sick, feed the hungry, protect peace among nations, and leave this world a better place.

The time has come for a new American emancipation—a great national drive to tear down economic barriers and liberate the spirit of enterprise in the most distressed areas of our country. My friends, together we can do this, and do it we must, so help me God.

From new freedom will spring new opportunities for growth, a more productive, fulfilled, and united people, and a stronger America—an America that will lead the technological revolution and also open its mind and heart and soul to the treasures of literature, music, and poetry, and the values of faith, courage, and love.

A dynamic economy, with more citizens working and paying taxes, will be our strongest tool to bring down budget deficits. But an almost unbroken fifty years of deficit spending has finally brought us to a time of reckoning. We have come to a turning point, a moment for hard decisions. I have asked the Cabinet and my staff a question, and now I put the same question to all of you: If not us, who? And if not now, when? It must be done by all of us going forward with a program aimed at reaching a balanced budget. We can then begin reducing the national debt.

I will shortly submit a budget to the Congress aimed at freezing government program spending for the next year. Beyond that, we must take further steps to permanently control government's power to tax and spend. We must act now to protect future generations from government's desire to spend its citizens' money and tax them into servitude when the bills come due. Let us make it unconstitutional for the federal government to spend more than the federal government takes in.

We have already started returning to the people and to state and local governments responsibilities better handled by them. Now, there is a place for the federal government in matters of social compassion. But our fundamental goals must be to reduce dependency and upgrade the dignity of those who are infirm or disadvantaged. And here a growing economy and support from family and community offer our best chance for a society where compassion is a way of life, where the old and infirm are cared for, the young and, yes, the unborn protected, and the unfortunate looked after and made self-sufficient.

And there is another area where the federal government can play a part. As an older American, I remember a time when people of different race, creed, or ethnic origin in our land found hatred and prejudice installed in social custom and, yes, in law. There is no story more heartening in our history than the progress that we have made toward the "brotherhood of man" that God intended for us. Let us resolve there will be no turning back or hesitation on the road to an America rich in dignity and abundant with opportunity for all our citizens.

Let us resolve that we the people will build an American opportunity society in which all of us—white and black, rich and poor, young and old—will go forward together arm in arm. Again, let us remember that though our heritage is one of bloodlines from every corner of the earth, we are all Americans pledged to carry on this last, best hope of man on earth.

I have spoken of our domestic goals and the limitations which we should put on our national government. Now let me turn to a task which is the primary responsibility of national government—the safety and security of our people.

Today, we utter no prayer more fervently than the ancient prayer for peace on earth. Yet history has shown that peace will not come, nor will our freedom be preserved, by good will alone. There are those in the world who scorn our vision of human dignity and freedom. One nation, the Soviet Union, has conducted the greatest military buildup in the history of man, building arsenals of awesome offensive weapons.

We have made progress in restoring our defense capability. But much remains to be done. There must be no wavering by us, nor any doubts by others, that America will meet her responsibilities to remain free, secure, and at peace.

There is only one way safely and legitimately to reduce the cost of national security, and that is to reduce the need for it. And this we are trying to do in negotiations with the Soviet Union. We are not just discussing limits on a further increase of nuclear weapons. We seek, instead, to reduce their number. We seek the total elimination one day of nuclear weapons from the face of the earth.

Now, for decades, we and the Soviets have lived under the threat of mutual assured destruction; if either resorted to the use of nuclear weapons, the other could retaliate and destroy the one who had started it. Is there either logic or morality in believing that if one side threatens to kill tens of millions of our people, our only recourse is to threaten killing tens of millions of theirs?

I have approved a research program to find, if we can, a security shield that would destroy nuclear missiles before they reach their target. It wouldn't kill people, it would destroy weapons. It wouldn't militarize space, it would help demilitarize the arsenals of earth. It would render nuclear weapons obsolete. We will meet with the Soviets, hoping that we can agree on a way to rid the world of the threat of nuclear destruction.

We strive for peace and security, heartened by the changes all around us. Since the turn of the century, the number of democracies in the world has grown fourfold. Human freedom is on the march, and nowhere more so than our own hemisphere. Freedom is one of the deepest and noblest aspirations of the human spirit. People worldwide hunger for the right of self-determination, for those inalienable rights that make for human dignity and progress.

America must remain freedom's staunchest friend, for freedom is our best ally.

And it is the world's only hope, to conquer poverty and preserve peace. Every blow we inflict against poverty will be a blow against its dark allies of oppression and war. Every victory for human freedom will be a victory for world peace.

So we go forward today, a nation still mighty in its youth and powerful in its purpose. With our alliances strengthened, with our economy leading the world to a new age of economic expansion, we look forward to a world rich in possibilities. And all this because we have worked and acted together, not as members of political parties, but as Americans.

My friends, we live in a world that is lit by lightning. So much is changing and will change, but so much endures, and transcends time.

History is a ribbon, always unfurling; history is a journey. And as we continue our journey, we think of those who traveled before us. We stand together again at the steps of this symbol of our democracy—or we would have been standing at the steps if it hadn't gotten so cold. Now we are standing inside this symbol of our democracy. Now we hear again the echoes of our past: a general falls to his knees in the hard snow of Valley Forge; a lonely president paces the darkened halls and ponders his struggle to preserve the Union; the men of the Alamo call out encouragement to each other; a settler pushes west and sings a song, and the song echoes out forever and fills the unknowing air.

It is the American sound. It is hopeful, big-hearted, idealistic, daring, decent, and fair. That's our heritage; that is our song. We sing it still. For all our problems, our differences, we are together as of old, as we raise our voices to the God who is the Author of this most tender music. And may He continue to hold us close as we fill the world with our sound—sound in unity, affection, and love—one people under God, dedicated to the dream of freedom that He has placed in the human heart, called upon now to pass that dream on to a waiting and hopeful world.

God bless you and may God bless America.

20

THE CHALLENGER
DISASTER

Millions watched what should have been another victory for the U.S. space program when this disaster unfolded. President Reagan was preparing for a lunch with media, normally held prior to the State of the Union address, when staffers notified him. He then watched the TV coverage with them. Later, Reagan would refer to this day as "one of the hardest days I ever spent in the Oval Office."

He gave the memorable 648 word speech at 5 p.m. Even Tip O'Neill who often sparred with Reagan said that he had seen the worst and the best of the President in just a few hours. O'Neil recalled, "It was a trying day for all Americans–and Ronald Reagan spoke to our highest ideals."

In the speech, Reagan observed, "I've always had great faith in and respect for our space program, and what happened today does nothing to diminish it."

Address to the Nation

———

Ladies and Gentlemen, I'd planned to speak to you tonight to report on the state of the Union, but the events of earlier today have led me to change those plans. Today is a day for mourning and remembering. Nancy and I are pained to the core by the tragedy of the shuttle Challenger. We know we share this pain with all of the people of our country. This is truly a national loss.

Nineteen years ago, almost to the day, we lost three astronauts in a terrible accident on the ground. But we've never lost an astronaut in flight; we've never had a tragedy like this. And perhaps we've forgotten the courage it took for the crew of the shuttle. But they, the Challenger Seven, were aware of the dangers, overcame them, and did their jobs brilliantly. We mourn seven heroes: Michael Smith, Dick Scobee, Judith Resnik, Ronald McNair, Ellison Onizuka, Gregory Jarvis, and Christa McAuliffe. We mourn their loss as a nation together.

[To] the families of the seven: we cannot bear, as you do, the full impact of this tragedy. But we feel the loss, and we're thinking about you so very much. Your loved ones were daring and brave, and they had that special grace, that special spirit that says, "Give me a challenge and I'll meet it with joy." They had a hunger to explore the universe and discover its truths. They wished to serve, and they did. They served all of us. We've grown used to wonders in this century; it's hard to dazzle us. But for twenty-five years the United States space program has been doing just that. We've grown used to the idea of space, and perhaps we forget that we've only just begun. We're still pioneers. They, the members of the Challenger crew, were pioneers.

And I want to say something to the schoolchildren of America who were watching the live coverage of the shuttle's takeoff. I know it is hard to understand, but sometimes painful things like this happen. It's all part of the process of exploration and discovery. It's all part of taking a chance and expanding man's horizons. The future doesn't belong to the fainthearted; it belongs to the brave. The Challenger crew was pulling us into the future, and we'll continue to follow them.

I've always had great faith in and respect for our space program, and what happened today does nothing to diminish it. We don't hide our space program. We don't keep secrets and cover things up. We do it all up front and in public. That's the way freedom is, and we wouldn't change it for a minute. We'll continue our quest in space. There will be more shuttle flights and more shuttle crews and, yes, more volunteers, more civilians, more teachers in space. Nothing ends here; our hopes and our journeys continue. I want to add that I wish I could talk to every man and woman who works for NASA or who worked on this mission and tell them: "Your dedication and professionalism have moved and impressed us for decades. And we know of your anguish. We share it."

There's a coincidence today. On this day 390 years ago, the great explorer Sir Francis Drake died aboard ship off the coast of Panama. In his lifetime the great frontiers were the oceans, and an historian later said, ""He lived by the sea, died on it, and was buried in it." Well, today we can say of the Challenger crew: Their dedication was, like Drake's, complete.

The crew of the space shuttle Challenger honored us by the manner in which they lived their lives. We will never forget them, nor the last time we saw them, this morning, as they prepared for their journey and waved goodbye and "slipped the surly bonds of earth" to "touch the face of God."

Thank you.

21

IRAN-CONTRA
CONTROVERSY

This was undoubtedly one of Reagan's more difficult speeches. He waited for three months before addressing what had become a damaging scandal related to allegations that he had authorized funds to be diverted from an arms deal with Iran to pay off Contra rebels for the release of U.S. hostages. Although the government investigation never proved that Reagan was aware of the proposed arrangements, several members of his administration including then-Defense Secretary Casper Weinberger were caught up in the scandal.

In the speech, Reagan explained that he would adopt the Tower board recommendations. He would bring on a new team of security advisors, a new CIA chief and would also order the National Security Council to review all covert operations.

Ever the optimist, Reagan refused to dwell on this tarnish, noting, "Now, what should happen when you make a mistake is this: You take your knocks, you learn your lessons, and then you move on."

Address to the Nation

MARCH 4, 1987

My fellow Americans:

I've spoken to you from this historic office on many occasions and about many things. The power of the presidency is often thought to reside within this Oval Office. Yet it doesn't rest here; it rests in you, the American people, and in your trust. Your trust is what gives a president his powers of leadership and his personal strength, and it's what I want to talk to you about this evening.

For the past three months I've been silent on the revelations about Iran. And you must have been thinking: "Well, why doesn't he tell us what's happening? Why doesn't he just speak to us as he has in the past when we've faced troubles or tragedies?" Others of you, I guess, were thinking: "What's he doing hiding out in the White House?" Well, the reason I haven't spoken to you before now is this: You deserve the truth. And as frustrating as the waiting has been, I felt it was improper to come to you with sketchy reports, or possibly even erroneous statements, which would then have to be corrected, creating even more doubt and confusion. There's been enough of that.

I've paid a price for my silence in terms of your trust and confidence. But I've had to wait, as you have, for the complete story. That's why I appointed Ambassador David Abshire as my special counselor to help get out the thousands of documents to the various investigations. And I appointed a special review board, the Tower board, which took on the chore of pulling the truth together for me and getting to the bottom of things. It has now issued its findings.

I'm often accused of being an optimist, and it's true I had to hunt pretty hard to find any good news in the board's report. As you know, it's well stocked with criticisms, which I'll discuss in a moment, but I was very relieved to read this sentence: "The Board is convinced that the president does indeed want the full story to be told." And that will continue to be my pledge to you as the other investigations go forward.

I want to thank the members of the panel: former Senator John Tower, former Secretary of State Edmund Muskie, and former national security adviser Brent Scowcroft. They have done the nation, as well as me personally, a great service by submitting a report of such integrity and depth. They have my genuine and enduring gratitude.

I've studied the board's report. Its findings are honest, convincing, and highly critical; and I accept them. And tonight I want to share with you my thoughts on these findings and report to you on the actions I'm taking to implement the board's recommendations.

First, let me say I take full responsibility for my own actions and for those of my administration. As angry as I may be about activities undertaken without my knowledge, I am still accountable for those activities. As disappointed as I may be in some who served me, I'm still the one who must answer to the American people for this behavior. And as personally distasteful as I find secret bank accounts and diverted funds—well, as the Navy would say, this happened on my watch.

Let's start with the part that is the most controversial. A few months ago I told the American people I did not trade arms for hostages. My heart and my best intentions still tell me that's true, but the facts and the evidence tell me it is not. As the Tower board reported, what began as a strategic opening to Iran deteriorated, in its implementation, into trading arms for hostages. This runs counter to my own beliefs, to administration policy, and to the original strategy we had in mind. There are reasons why it happened, but no excuses. It was a mistake.

I undertook the original Iran initiative in order to develop relations with those who might assume leadership in a post-Khomeini government. It's clear from the board's report, however, that I let my personal concern for the hostages spill over into the geopolitical strategy of reaching out to Iran. I asked so many questions about the hostages' welfare that I didn't ask enough about the specifics of the total Iran plan.

Let me say to the hostage families: We have not given up. We never will. And I promise you we'll use every legitimate means to free your loved ones from captivity. But I must also caution that those Americans who freely remain in such dangerous areas must know that they're responsible for their own safety.

Now, another major aspect of the board's findings regards the transfer of funds to the Nicaraguan contras. The Tower board wasn't able to find out what happened to this money, so the facts here will be left to the continuing investigations of the court-appointed independent counsel and the two congressional investigating committees. I'm confident the truth will come out about this matter, as well. As I told the Tower board, I didn't know about any diversion of funds to the contras. But as president, I cannot escape responsibility.

Much has been said about my management style, a style that's worked successfully for me during eight years as governor of California and for most of my presidency. The way I work is to identify the problem, find the right individuals to do the job, and then let them go to it. I've found this invariably brings out the best in people. They seem to rise to their full capability, and in the long run you get more done.

When it came to managing the NSC staff, let's face it: my style didn't match its previous track record. I've already begun correcting this. As a start, yesterday I met with the entire professional staff of the National Security Council. I defined for them the values I want to guide the national security policies of this country. I told them that I wanted a policy that was as justifiable and understandable in public as it was in secret. I wanted a policy that reflected the will of the Congress as well as of the White House. And I told them that there will be no more freelancing by individuals when it comes to our national security.

You've heard a lot about the staff of the National Security Council in recent months. Well, I can tell you, they are good and dedicated government employees, who put in long hours for the nation's benefit. They are eager and anxious to serve their country.

One thing still upsetting me, however, is that no one kept proper records of meetings or decisions. This led to my failure to recollect whether I approved an arms shipment before or after the fact. I did approve it; I just can't say specifically when. Well, rest assured, there's plenty of record keeping now going on at 1600 Pennsylvania Avenue.

For nearly a week now, I've been studying the board's report. I want the American people to know that this wrenching ordeal of recent months has not been in vain. I endorse every one of the Tower board's recommendations. In fact, I'm going beyond its recommendations so as to put the house in even better order.

I'm taking action in three basic areas: personnel, national security policy, and the process for making sure that the system works. First, personnel. I've brought in an accomplished and highly respected new team here at the White House. They bring new blood, new energy, and new credibility and experience.

Former Senator Howard Baker, my new chief of staff, possesses a breadth of legislative and foreign affairs skills that's impossible to match. I'm hopeful that his experience as minority and majority leader of the Senate can help us forge a new partnership with the Congress, especially on foreign and national security policies. I'm genuinely honored that he's given up his own presidential aspirations to serve the country as my chief of staff.

Frank Carlucci, my new national security adviser, is respected for his experience in government and trusted for his judgment and counsel. Under him, the NSC staff is being rebuilt with proper

management discipline. Already, almost half the NSC professional staff is comprised of new people.

Yesterday I nominated William Webster, a man of sterling rep-
utation, to be Director of the Central Intelligence Agency. Mr.
Webster has served as Director of the FBI and as a U.S. District
Court judge. He understands the meaning of "rule of law."

So that his knowledge of national security matters can be available to me on a continuing basis, I will also appoint John Tower
to serve as a member of my Foreign Intelligence Advisory Board.
I am considering other changes in personnel, and I'll move more
furniture, as I see fit, in the weeks and months ahead.

Second, in the area of national security policy, I have ordered
the NSC to begin a comprehensive review of all covert operations. I have also directed that any covert activity be in support of clear policy objectives and in compliance with American
values. I expect a covert policy that if Americans saw it on the
front page of their newspaper, they'd say, "That makes sense." I
have issued a directive prohibiting the NSC staff itself from undertaking covert operations—no ifs, ands, or buts. I have asked
Vice President Bush to reconvene his task force on terrorism
to review our terrorist policy in light of the events that have
occurred.

Third, in terms of the process of reaching national security decisions, I am adopting in total the Tower report's model of how
the NSC process and staff should work. I am directing Mr. Carlucci to take the necessary steps to make that happen. He will
report back to me on further reforms that might be needed. I've
created the post of NSC legal adviser to assure a greater sensitiv-
ity to matters of law.

I am also determined to make the congressional oversight process work. Proper procedures for consultation with the Congress
will be followed, not only in letter but in spirit Before the end of
March, I will report to the Congress on all the steps I've taken in
line with the Tower board's conclusions.

Now, what should happen when you make a mistake is this: You take your knocks, you learn your lessons, and then you move on. That's the healthiest way to deal with a problem. This in no way diminishes the importance of the other continuing investigations, but the business of our country and our people must proceed. I've gotten this message from Republicans and Democrats in Congress, from allies around the world, and—if we're reading the signals right—even from the Soviets. And of course, I've heard the message from you, the American people. You know, by the time you reach my age, you've made plenty of mistakes. And if you've lived your life properly—so, you learn. You put things in perspective. You pull your energies together. You change. You go forward.

My fellow Americans, I have a great deal that I want to accomplish with you and for you over the next two years. And the Lord willing, that's exactly what I intend to do.

Good night, and God bless you.

22

"Mr. Gorbachev, Tear Down This Wall!"

Throughout our country's history, the occasional president has spoken a line that captures the spirit of his service. On June 12, 1987, while addressing the German people at the Brandenburg Gate, Ronald Reagan did just that.

Reagan's 1987 Address at the Brandenburg Gate was the culmination of six years in office defined by Cold War politics. While the crux of the speech was to commemorate the 750th anniversary of Berlin, Reagan spoke out against communist oppression. He bonded with his audience, using phrases like "Berliner Schnauze"–a rough dialect combining humor and gruffness–to capture their ear and elicit a chuckle. Albeit out of sight, he spoke directly to East Berliners as if they were on the west side of the Wall. And though many of his aides advised him to leave the now infamous line out of the speech, Reagan thought it best not to mince words. "Mr. Gorbachev, tear down this wall!" he implored.

Speech at the Brandenburg Gate, West Berlin

JUNE 12, 1987

Chancellor Kohl, Governing Mayor Diepgen, ladies and gentlemen:

Twenty-four years ago, President John F. Kennedy visited Berlin, speaking to the people of this city and the world at the city hall. Well, since then two other presidents have come, each in his turn, to Berlin. And today, I, myself, make my second visit to your city.

We come to Berlin, we American presidents, because it's our duty to speak, in this place, of freedom. But I must confess, we're drawn here by other things as well: by the feeling of history in this city, more than five hundred years older than our own nation; by the beauty of the Grunewald and the Tiergarten; most of all, by your courage and determination.

Perhaps the composer Paul Lincke understood something about American presidents. You see, like so many presidents before me, I come here today because wherever I go, whatever I do: "Ich hab noch einen Koffer in Berlin." [I still have a suitcase in Berlin.]

Our gathering today is being broadcast throughout Western Europe and North America. I understand that it is being seen and heard as well in the East. To those listening in East Berlin, a special word: Although I cannot be with you, I address my remarks to you just as surely as to those standing here before me. For I join you, as I join your fellow countrymen in the West, in this firm, this unalterable belief: Es gibt nur ein Berlin. [There is only one Berlin.]

Behind me stands a wall that encircles the free sectors of this city, part of a vast system of barriers that divides the entire continent of Europe. From the Baltic south, those barriers cut across Germany in a gash of barbed wire, concrete, dog runs, and guard towers. Farther south, there may be no visible, no obvious wall. But there remain armed guards and checkpoints all the same— still a restriction on the right to travel, still an instrument to impose upon ordinary men and women the will of a totalitarian state. Yet it is here in Berlin where the wall emerges most clearly: here, cutting across your city, where the news photo and the television screen have imprinted this brutal division of a continent upon the mind of the world. Standing before the Brandenburg Gate, every man is a German, separated from his fellow men. Every man is a Berliner, forced to look upon a scar.

President von Weizsacker has said, "The German question is open as long as the Brandenburg Gate is closed." Today I say: As long as the gate is closed, as long as this scar of a wall is permitted to stand, it is not the German question alone that remains open, but the question of freedom for all mankind. Yet I do not come here to lament. For I find in Berlin a message of hope; even in the shadow of this wall, a message of triumph.

In this season of spring in 1945, the people of Berlin emerged from their aid-raid shelters to find devastation. Thousands of miles away, the people of the United States reached out to help. And in 1947 Secretary of State—as you've been told—George Marshall announced the creation of what would become known as the Marshall Plan. Speaking precisely forty years ago this month, he said: "Our policy is directed not against any country or doctrine, but against hunger, poverty, desperation, and chaos."

In the Reichstag a few moments ago, I saw a display commemorating this fortieth anniversary of the Marshall Plan. I was struck by the sign on a burnt-out, gutted structure that was being rebuilt. I understand that Berliners of my own generation can remember seeing signs like it dotted throughout the western sectors of the city. The sign read simply: "The Marshall Plan is helping here to strengthen the free world." A strong, free world in the West. That dream became real. Japan rose from ruin to become an economic giant. Italy, France, Belgium—virtually every nation in Western

Europe saw political and economic rebirth; the European Community was founded.

In West Germany and here in Berlin, there took place an economic miracle, the Wirtschaftswunder. Adenauer, Erhard, Reuter, and other leaders understood the practical importance of liberty—that just as truth can flourish only when the journalist is given freedom of speech, so prosperity can come about only when the farmer and businessman enjoy economic freedom. The German leaders reduced tariffs, expanded free trade, lowered taxes. From 1950 to 1960 alone, the standard of living in West Germany and Berlin doubled.

Where four decades ago there was rubble, today in West Berlin there is the greatest industrial output of any city in Germany— busy office blocks, fine homes and apartments, proud avenues, and the spreading lawns of parkland. Where a city's culture seemed to have been destroyed, today there are two great universities, orchestras and an opera, countless theaters, and museums. Where there was want, today there is abundance—food, clothing, automobiles—the wonderful goods of the Ku'damm. From devastation, from utter ruin, you Berliners have, in freedom, rebuilt a city that once again ranks as one of the greatest on earth. The Soviets may have had other plans; but, my friends, there were a few things the Soviets didn't count on—Berliner Herz, Berliner Humor, ja, und Berliner Schnauze. [Berliner heart, Berliner humor, yes, and a Berliner schnauze.] [Laughter]

In the 1950s, Khrushchev predicted: "We will bury you." But in the West today, we see a free world that has achieved a level of prosperity and well-being unprecedented in all human history. In the Communist world, we see failure, technological backwardness, declining standards of health, even want of the most basic kind: too little food. Even today, the Soviet Union still cannot feed itself. After these four decades, then, there stands before the entire world one great and inescapable conclusion: Freedom leads to prosperity. Freedom replaces the ancient

hatreds among the nations with comity and peace. Freedom is
the victor.

And now the Soviets themselves may, in a limited way, be
coming to understand the importance of freedom. We hear much
from Moscow about a new policy of reform and openness. Some
political prisoners have been released. Certain foreign news
broadcasts are no longer being jammed. Some economic enter-
prises have been permitted to operate with greater freedom from
state control.

Are these the beginnings of profound changes in the Soviet
state? Or are they token gestures, intended to raise false hopes in
the West, or to strengthen the Soviet system without changing
it? We welcome change and openness; for we believe that freedom and security go together, that the advance of human liberty
can only strengthen the cause of world peace. There is one sign
the Soviets can make that would be unmistakable, that would advance dramatically the cause of freedom and peace.

General Secretary Gorbachev, if you seek peace, if you seek
prosperity for the Soviet Union and Eastern Europe, if you seek
liberalization: Come here to this gate! Mr. Gorbachev, open this
gate! Mr. Gorbachev, tear down this wall!

I understand the fear of war and the pain of division that afflict
this continent—and I pledge to you my country's efforts to help
overcome these burdens. To be sure, we in the West must resist
Soviet expansion, so we must maintain defenses of unassailable
strength. Yet we seek peace, so we must strive to reduce arms on
both sides.

Beginning ten years ago, the Soviets challenged the Western
alliance with a grave new threat, hundreds of new and more
deadly SS-20 nuclear missiles capable of striking every capital
in Europe. The Western alliance responded by committing itself
to a counter-deployment unless the Soviets agreed to negotiate
a better solution, namely, the elimination of such weapons on
both sides. For many months, the Soviets refused to bargain in

earnestness. As the alliance, in turn, prepared to go forward with its counter-deployment, there were difficult days—days of protests like those during my 1982 visit to this city—and the Soviets later walked away from the table.

But through it all, the alliance held firm. And I invite those who protested then—I invite those who protest today—to mark this fact: Because we remained strong, the Soviets came back to the table.

And because we remained strong, today we have within reach the possibility, not merely of limiting the growth of arms, but of eliminating, for the first time, an entire class of nuclear weapons from the face of the earth.

As I speak, NATO ministers are meeting in Iceland to review the progress of our proposals for eliminating these weapons. At the talks in Geneva, we have also proposed deep cuts in strategic offensive weapons. And the Western allies have likewise made far-reaching proposals to reduce the danger of conventional war and to place a total ban on chemical weapons.

While we pursue these arms reductions, I pledge to you that we will maintain the capacity to deter Soviet aggression at any level at which it might occur. And in cooperation with many of our allies, the United States is pursuing the Strategic Defense Initiative—research to base deterrence not on the threat of offensive retaliation, but on defenses that truly defend; on systems, in short, that will not target populations, but shield them. By these means we seek to increase the safety of Europe and all the world. But we must remember a crucial fact: East and West do not mistrust each other because we are armed; we are armed because we mistrust each other. And our differences are not about weapons but about liberty. When President Kennedy spoke at the city hall those twenty-four years ago, freedom was encircled, Berlin was under siege. And today, despite all the pressures upon this city, Berlin stands secure in its liberty. And freedom itself is transforming the globe.

In the Philippines, in South and Central America, democracy has been given a rebirth. Throughout the Pacific, free markets are working miracle after miracle of economic growth. In the industrialized nations, a technological revolution is taking place—a revolution marked by rapid, dramatic advances in computers and telecommunications.

In Europe, only one nation and those it controls refuse to join the community of freedom. Yet in this age of redoubled economic growth, of information and innovation, the Soviet Union faces a choice: It must make fundamental changes, or it will become obsolete.

Today thus represents a moment of hope. We in the West stand ready to cooperate with the East to promote true openness, to break down barriers that separate people, to create a safe, freer world. And surely there is no better place than Berlin, the meeting place of East and West, to make a start. Free people of Berlin: Today, as in the past, the United States stands for the strict observance and full implementation of all parts of the Four Power Agreement of 1971. Let us use this occasion, the 750th anniversary of this city, to usher in a new era, to seek a still fuller, richer life for the Berlin of the future. Together, let us maintain and develop the ties between the Federal Republic and the Western sectors of Berlin, which is permitted by the 1971 agreement.

And I invite Mr. Gorbachev: Let us work to bring the Eastern and Western parts of the city closer together, so that all the inhabitants of all Berlin can enjoy the benefits that come with life in one of the great cities of the world.

To open Berlin still further to all Europe, East and West, let us expand the vital air access to this city, finding ways of making commercial air service to Berlin more convenient, more comfortable, and more economical. We look to the day when West Berlin can become one of the chief aviation hubs in all central Europe.

With our French and British partners, the United States is prepared to help bring international meetings to Berlin. It would be only fitting for Berlin to serve as the site of United Nations meetings, or world conferences on human rights and arms control or other issues that call for international cooperation.

There is no better way to establish hope for the future than to enlighten young minds, and we would be honored to sponsor summer youth exchanges, cultural events, and other programs for young Berliners from the East. Our French and British friends, I'm certain, will do the same. And it's my hope that an authority can be found in East Berlin to sponsor visits from young people of the Western sectors.

One final proposal, one close to my heart: Sport represents a source of enjoyment and ennoblement, and you may have noted that the Republic of Korea—South Korea—has offered to permit certain events of the 1988 Olympics to take place in the North. International sports competitions of all kinds could take place in both parts of this city. And what better way to demonstrate to the world the openness of this city than to offer in some future year to hold the Olympic games here in Berlin, East and West?

In these four decades, as I have said, you Berliners have built a great city. You've done so in spite of threats—the Soviet attempts to impose the East-mark, the blockade. Today the city thrives in spite of the challenges implicit in the very presence of this wall. What keeps you here? Certainly there's a great deal to be said for your fortitude, for your defiant courage. But I believe there's something deeper, something that involves Berlin's whole look and feel and way of life—not mere sentiment. No one could live long in Berlin without being completely disabused of illusions. Something, instead, that has seen the difficulties of life in Berlin but chose to accept them, that continues to build this good and proud city in contrast to a surrounding totalitarian presence, that refuses to release human energies or aspirations. Something that speaks with a powerful voice of affirmation, that says yes to this city, yes to the future, yes to freedom. In a word, I would submit that what keeps you in Berlin is love—love both profound and abiding.

Perhaps this gets to the root of the matter, to the most fundamental distinction of all between East and West. The totalitarian world produces backwardness because it does such violence to the spirit, thwarting the human impulse to create, to enjoy, to worship. The totalitarian world finds even symbols of love and of worship an affront. Years ago, before the East Germans began rebuilding their churches, they erected a secular structure: the television tower at Alexander Platz. Virtually ever since, the authorities have been working to correct what they view as the tower's one major flaw, treating the glass sphere at the top with paints and chemicals of every kind. Yet, even today when the sun strikes that sphere—that sphere that towers over all Berlin—the light makes the sign of the cross. There in Berlin, like the city itself, symbols of love, symbols of worship, cannot be suppressed.

As I looked out a moment ago from the Reichstag, that embodiment of German unity, I noticed words crudely spray-painted upon the wall, perhaps by a young Berliner: "This wall will fall. Beliefs become reality." Yes, across Europe, this wall will fall. For it cannot withstand faith; it cannot withstand truth. The wall cannot withstand freedom.

And I would like, before I close, to say one word. I have read, and I have been questioned since I've been here, about certain demonstrations against my coming. And I would like to say just one thing, and to those who demonstrate so. I wonder if they have ever asked themselves that if they should have the kind of government they apparently seek, no one would ever be able to do what they're doing again. Thank you and God bless you all.

23

FAREWELL ADDRESS

Looking back over his eight years in office, Reagan discussed the economic recovery and the recovery of American morale. He is clearly proud of the renewed patriotism and he calls the U.S. a "shining city on a hill."

But Reagan cautioned, "This national feeling is good, but it won't count for much, and it won't last, unless it's grounded in thoughtfulness and knowledge." He went on to urge people to make certain that children understand what it means to be an American and that they're taught history based on what's important, not just in fashion.

Reagan's tone is both simple and personal. He talks about walking upstairs in the White House and looking outside at the monuments. His language is simple, strong and occasionally collo-quial. And the great communicator ends on an upbeat note by saying, "My friends: We did it. We weren't just marking time. We made a difference."

Address to the Nation

JANUARY 11, 1989

———

B efore I say my formal goodbye, maybe I should tell you what I'm up to now that I'm out of office. Well, I'm still giving speeches, still sounding off about those things I didn't get accomplished while I was president.

High on my agenda are three things. First, I'm out there stumping to help future presidents—Republican or Democrat—get those tools they need to bring the budget under control. And those tools are a line-item veto and a constitutional amendment to balance the budget. Second, I'm out there talking up the need to do something about political gerrymandering. This is the practice of rigging the boundaries of congressional districts. It is the greatest single blot on the integrity of our nation's electoral system, and it's high time we did something about it. And third, I'm talking up the idea of repealing the Twenty-second Amendment to the Constitution, the amendment that prevents a president from serving more than two terms. I believe it's a preemption of the people's right to vote for whomever they want as many times as they want.

So I'm back where I came in—out there on the mashed potato circuit. I have a feeling I'll be giving speeches until I'm called to the great beyond and maybe even after. All it will take is for St. Peter to say, "Ronald Wilson Reagan, what do you have to say for yourself? Speak up."

"Well, sir, unaccustomed as I am."

This is the thirty-fourth time I'll speak to you from the Oval Office and the last. We've been together eight years now, and soon it'll be time for me to go. But before I do, I wanted to share some thoughts, some of which I've been saving for a long time.

It's been the honor of my life to be your president. So many of you have written the past few weeks to say thanks, but I could say as much to you. Nancy and I are grateful for the opportunity you gave us to serve.

One of the things about the presidency is that you're always somewhat apart. You spent a lot of time going by too fast in a car someone else is driving, and seeing the people through tinted glass—the parents holding up a child, and the wave you saw too late and couldn't return. And so many times I wanted to stop and reach out from behind the glass, and connect. Well, maybe I can do a little of that tonight.

People ask how I feel about leaving. And the fact is, 'parting is such sweet sorrow.' The sweet part is California and the ranch and freedom, the sorrow the goodbyes, of course, and leaving this beautiful place.

You know, down the hall and up the stairs from this office is the part of the White House where the president and his family live. There are a few favorite windows I have up there that I like to stand and look out of early in the morning. The view is over the grounds here to the Washington Monument, and then the Mall and the Jefferson Memorial. But on mornings when the humidity is low, you can see past the Jefferson to the river, the Potomac, and the Virginia shore. Someone said that's the view Lincoln had when he saw the smoke rising from the Battle of Bull Run. I see more prosaic things: the grass on the banks, the morning traffic as people make their way to work, now and then a sailboat on the river.

I've been thinking a bit at that window. I've been reflecting on what the past eight years have meant and mean. And the image that comes to mind like a refrain is a nautical one—a small story about a big ship, and a refugee, and a sailor. It was back in the early eighties, at the height of the boat people. And the sailor was hard at work on the carrier Midway, which was patrolling the South China Sea. The sailor, like most American servicemen, was young, smart, and fiercely observant. The crew spied on the horizon a leaky little boat, and crammed inside were refugees from Indochina hoping to get to America. The Midway sent a small launch to bring them to the ship and safety. As the refugees made their way through the choppy seas, one spied the sailor on deck, and stood up, and called out to him. He yelled, "Hello, American sailor."

"Hello, freedom man."

A small moment with a big meaning, a moment the sailor, who wrote it in a letter, couldn't get out of his mind. And, when I saw it, neither could I. Because that's what it was to be an American in the 1980s. We stood, again, for freedom. I know we always have, but in the past few years the world again—and in a way, we ourselves—rediscovered it.

It's been quite a journey this decade, and we held together through some stormy seas. And at the end, together, we are reaching our destination.

The fact is, from Grenada to the Washington and Moscow summits, from the recession of '81 to '82, to the expansion that began in late '82 and continues to this day, we've made a difference. The way I see it, there were two great triumphs, two things that I'm proudest of. One is the economic recovery, in which the people of America created—and filled—19 million new jobs. The other is the recovery of our morale. America is respected again in the world and looked to for leadership.

Something that happened to me a few years ago reflects some of this. It was back in 1981, and I was attending my first big economic summit, which was held that year in Canada. The meeting place rotates among the member countries. The opening meeting was a formal dinner of the heads of government of the seven industrialized nations. Now, I sat there like the new kid in school and listened, and it was all Francois this and Helmut that. They dropped titles and spoke to one another on a first-name basis. Well, at one point I sort of leaned in and said, "My name's Ron." Well, in that same year, we began the actions we felt would ignite an economic comeback—cut taxes and regulation, started to cut spending. And soon the recovery began.

Two years later, another economic summit with pretty much the same cast. At the big opening meeting we all got together, and all of a sudden, just for a moment, I saw that everyone was just sitting there looking at me. And then one of them broke the silence. "Tell us about the American miracle," he said.

Well, back in 1980 when I was running for president, it was all so different. Some pundits said our programs would result in catastrophe. Our views on foreign affairs would cause war. Our plans for the economy would cause inflation to soar and bring about economic collapse. I even remember one highly respected economist saying, back in 1982, that "the engines of economic growth have shut down here, and they're likely to stay that way for years to come." Well, he and the other opinion leaders were wrong. The fact is what they called 'radical' was really 'right.' What they called 'dangerous' was just 'desperately needed.'

And in all of that time I won a nickname, 'The Great Communicator.' But I never thought it was my style or the words I used that made a difference. It was the content. I wasn't a great communicator, but I communicated great things, and they didn't spring full bloom from my brow, they came from the heart of a great nation—from our experience, our wisdom, and our belief in the principles that have guided us for two centuries. They called it the Reagan revolution. Well, I'll accept that, but for me it always seemed more like the great rediscovery, a rediscovery of our values and our common sense.

Common sense told us that when you put a big tax on something, the people will produce less of it. So we cut the people's tax rates, and the people produced more than ever before. The economy bloomed like a plant that had been cut back and could now grow quicker and stronger. Our economic program brought about the longest peacetime expansion in our history: real family income up, the poverty rate down, entrepreneurship booming,

and an explosion in research and new technology. We're exporting more than ever because American industry became more
competitive and at the same time, we summoned the national
will to knock down protectionist walls abroad instead of erecting
them at home.

Common sense also told us that to preserve the peace, we'd
have to become strong again after years of weakness and confusion. So we rebuilt our defenses, and this New Year we toasted
the new peacefulness around the globe. Not only have the su-
perpowers actually begun to reduce their stockpiles of nuclear
weapons—and hope for even more progress is bright—but the
regional conflicts that rack the globe are also beginning to cease.
The Persian Gulf is no longer a war zone. The Soviets are leaving
Afghanistan. The Vietnamese are preparing to pull out of Cambodia, and an American-mediated accord will soon send fifty thousand Cuban troops home from Angola.

The lesson of all this was, of course, that because we're a great
nation, our challenges seem complex. It will always be this way.
But as long as we remember our first principles and believe in
ourselves, the future will always be ours. And something else
we learned: Once you begin a great movement, there's no telling
where it will end. We meant to change a nation, and instead, we
changed a world.

Countries across the globe are turning to free markets and
free speech and turning away from the ideologies of the past. For
them, the great rediscovery of the 1980s has been that, lo and
behold, the moral way of government is the practical way of government. Democracy, the profoundly good, is also the profoundly
productive.

When you've got to the point when you can celebrate the an-
niversaries of your thirty-ninth birthday, you can sit back sometimes, review your life, and see it flowing before you. For me there
was a fork in the river, and it was right in the middle of my life. I
never meant to go into politics. It wasn't my intention when I was

young. But I was raised to believe you had to pay your way for the blessings bestowed on you. I was happy with my career in the entertainment world, but I ultimately went into politics because I wanted to protect something precious.

Ours was the first revolution in the history of mankind that truly reversed the course of government, and with three little words: We the People. "We the People" tell the government what to do; it doesn't tell us.

"We the People" are the driver; the government is the car. And we decide where it should go, and by what route, and how fast. Almost all the world's constitutions are documents in which governments tell the people what their privileges are. Our Constitution is a document in which "We the People" tell the government what it is allowed to do. "We the People" are free. This belief has been the underlying basis for everything I've tried to do these past eight years.

But back in the 1960s, when I began, it seemed to me that we'd begun reversing the order of things—that through more and more rules and regulations and confiscatory taxes, the government was taking more of our money, more of our options, and more of our freedom. I went into politics in part to put up my hand and say, "Stop." I was a citizen politician, and it seemed the right thing for a citizen to do.

I think we have stopped a lot of what needed stopping. And I hope we have once again reminded people that man is not free unless government is limited. There's a clear cause and effect here that is as neat and predictable as a law of physics: As government expands, liberty contracts.

Nothing is less free than pure Communism—and yet we have, the past few years, forged a satisfying new closeness with the Soviet Union. I've been asked if this isn't a gamble, and my answer is no, because we're basing our actions not on words but deeds. The detente of the 1970s was based not on actions but promises. They'd promise to treat their own people and the people of the world better. But the gulag was still the gulag, and the state was still expansionist, and they still waged proxy wars in Africa, Asia, and Latin America.

Well, this time, so far, it's different. President Gorbachev has brought about some internal democratic reforms and begun the withdrawal from Afghanistan. He has also freed prisoners whose names I've given him every time we've met.

But life has a way of reminding you of big things through small incidents. Once, during the heady days of the Moscow summit, Nancy and I decided to break off from the entourage one afternoon to visit the shops on Arbat Street—that's a little street just off Moscow's main shopping area. Even though our visit was a surprise, every Russian there immediately recognized us and called out our names and reached for our hands. We were just about swept away by the warmth. You could almost feel the possibilities in all that joy. But within seconds, a KGB detail pushed their way toward us and began pushing and shoving the people in the crowd. It was an interesting moment. It reminded me that while the man on the street in the Soviet Union yearns for peace, the government is Communist. And those who run it are Communists, and that means we and they view such issues as freedom and human rights very differently.

We must keep up our guard, but we must also continue to work together to lessen and eliminate tension and mistrust. My view is that President Gorbachev is different from previous Soviet leaders. I think he knows some of the things wrong with his society and is trying to fix them. We wish him well. And we'll continue to work to make sure that the Soviet Union that eventually emerges from this process is a less threatening one. What it all boils down to is this: I want the new closeness to continue. And it will, as long as we make it clear that we will continue to act in a certain way as long as they continue to act in a helpful manner. If and when they don't, at first pull your punches. If they persist, pull the plug. It's still trust by verify. It's still play, but cut the cards. It's still watch closely and don't be afraid to see what you see.

I've been asked if I have any regrets. Well, I do. The deficit is one. I've been talking a great deal about that lately, but tonight isn't for arguments, and I'm going to hold my tongue. But an observation: I've had my share of victories in the Congress, but what few people noticed is that I never won anything you didn't win for me. They never saw my troops, they never saw Reagan's regiments, the American people. You won every battle with every call you made and letter you wrote demanding action. Well, action is still needed if we're to finish the job. Reagan's regiments will have to become the Bush brigades. Soon he'll be the chief, and he'll need you every bit as much as I did.

Finally, there is a great tradition of warnings in presidential farewells, and I've got one that's been on my mind for some time. But oddly enough it starts with one of the things I'm proudest of in the past eight years: the resurgence of national pride that I call the new patriotism. This national feeling is good, but it won't count for much, and it won't last, unless it's grounded in thoughtfulness and knowledge.

An informed patriotism is what we want. And are we doing a good enough job teaching our children what America is and what she represents in the long history of the world? Those of us who are over thirty-five or so years of age grew up in a different America. We were taught, very directly, what it means to be an American. And we absorbed, almost in the air, a love of country and an appreciation of its institutions. If you didn't get these things from your family, you got them from the neighborhood, from the father down the street who fought in Korea or the family who lost someone at Anzio. Or you could get a sense of patriotism from school. And if all else failed, you could get a sense of patriotism from the popular culture. The movies celebrated democratic values and implicitly reinforced the idea that America was special. TV was like that, too, through the mid-sixties.

But now, we're about to enter the nineties, and some things have changed. Younger parents aren't sure that an unambivalent appreciation of America is the right thing to teach modern children. And as for those who create the popular culture, well-grounded patriotism is no longer the style. Our spirit is back, but we haven't reinstitutionalized it. We've got to do a better job of getting across that America is freedom—freedom of speech, freedom of religion, freedom of enterprise. And freedom is special and rare. It's fragile; it needs protection.

So we've got to teach history based not on what's in fashion but what's important—why the Pilgrims came here, who Jimmy Doolittle was, and what those thirty seconds over Tokyo meant. You know, four years ago, on the fortieth anniversary of D-day, I read a letter from a young woman writing to her late father, who'd fought on Omaha Beach. Her name was Lisa Zanatta Henn, and she said, "We will always remember, we will never forget what the boys of Normandy did." Well, let's help her keep her word. If we forget what we did, we won't know who we are. I'm warning of an eradication of the American memory that could result, ultimately, in an erosion of the American spirit. Let's start with some basics: more attention to American history and a greater emphasis on civic ritual.

And let me offer lesson number one about America: All great change in America begins at the dinner table. So, tomorrow night in the kitchen I hope the talking begins. And children, if your parents haven't been teaching you what it means to be an American, let 'em know and nail 'em on it. That would be a very American thing to do.

And that's about all I have to say tonight, except for one thing. The past few days when I've been at that window upstairs, I've thought a bit of the 'shining city upon a hill.' The phrase comes from John Winthrop, who wrote it to describe the America he imagined. What he imagined was important because he was an early Pilgrim, an early freedom man. He journeyed here on what today we'd call a little wooden boat, and like the other Pilgrims, he was looking for a home that would be free. I've spoken of the shining city all my political life, but I don't know if I ever quite communicated what I saw when I said it. But in my mind it was a tall, proud city built on rocks stronger than oceans, windswept, God-blessed, and teeming with people of all kinds living in harmony and peace; a city with free ports that hummed with commerce and creativity. And if there had to be city walls, the walls had doors and the doors were open to anyone with the will and the heart to get here. That's how I saw it, and see it still.

And how stands the city on this winter night? More prosperous, more secure, and happier than it was eight years ago. But more than that: After two hundred years, two centuries, she still stands strong and true on the granite ridge, and her glow has held steady no matter what storm. And she's still a beacon, still a magnet for all who must have freedom, for all the pilgrims from all the lost places who are hurtling through the darkness, toward home.

We've done our part. And as I walk off into the city streets, a final word to the men and women of the Reagan revolution, the men and women across America who for eight years did the work that brought America back. My friends: We did it. We weren't just marking time. We made a difference. We made the city stronger, we made the city freer, and we left her in good hands. All in all, not bad, not bad at all.

And so, goodbye, God bless you, and God bless the United States of America.

24

RONALD REAGAN ON THE COLD WAR

Speaking at the dedication of a sculpture celebrating Winston Churchill, Reagan talked affectionately of Churchill who he dubbed "the greatest communicator of our time." But Reagan also used the occasion to mark the year anniversary of the demise of the Berlin Wall. And he ties that event to the goals and beliefs of Churchill who frequently warned about the dangerous powers of Hitler during the World War II.

"Ours is a more peaceful planet because of men like Churchill and Truman and countless others who shared their dream of a world where no one wields a sword and no one drags a chain," said Reagan.

He went on to discuss his own experience as president, having to fight the Soviet leaders and the development of nuclear and other weapons. Always looking to the future, Reagan observed, "Soviet Russia is coming out of the dark to join the family of nations. How pleased Sir Winston would be!"

Westminster College Cold War Memorial, Fulton, Missouri

NOVEMBER 19, 1990

I can hardly visit this magnificent setting, so rich in memory and symbolism, without recalling the comment Sir Winston Churchill made when he was congratulated on the size of an audience gathered to hear him speak. Any other politician would have been flattered. Not Churchill. It was no great achievement to draw a crowd, he said. Twice as many would have turned out for a public hanging.

Maybe so, but I am deeply grateful to each of you for your warm welcome. What an honor it is for me to come to Fulton—indelibly stamped with the name and eloquence of Churchill. What a privilege to be on hand to help dedicate Edwina Sandys' sculpture celebrating the triumph of her grandfather's principles. And what a source of pride to receive an honorary degree from this distinguished college, whose illustrious past is equaled only by its future promise.

Today we rejoice in the demise of the Berlin Wall that was permanently breached just one year ago.

We remember brave men and women on both sides of the Iron Curtain who devoted their lives—and sometimes sacrificed them—so that we might inhabit a world without barriers. And we recall with the intensity born of shared struggles the greatest Briton of them all, a child of parliamentary democracy who boasted of an American mother and who therefore claimed to be an English-speaking union all by himself.

Who standing here beside this magnificent twelfth-century church that commemorated Sir Winston's 1946 visit can ever forget the indomitable figure with the bulldog expression and the upthrust 'V' for victory?

As the greatest communicator of our time, Sir Winston enlisted the English language itself in the battle against Hitler and his hateful doctrines. When the Nazi might prevailed from Warsaw to the Channel Islands and from Egypt to the Arctic Ocean, at a time when the whole cause of human liberty stood trembling and imperiled, he breathed defiance in phrases that will ring down through centuries to come.

And when the guns at last fell silent in the spring of 1945, no man on earth had done more to preserve civilization during the hour of its greatest trial.

Near the end of World War II, but before the election that everyone knew must follow V-E Day, *The Times of London* prepared an editorial suggesting that Prime Minister Churchill run as a nonpartisan figure, above the fray of parliamentary politics, and that he gracefully retire soon after to rest on his laurels and bask in the glow of yesterday's triumph.

The editor informed Sir Winston of both points he intended to make. Churchill had a ready reply. As for the first suggestion: "Mr. Editor," he said, "I fight for my corner." And as for the second: "Mr. Editor, I leave when the pub closes."

For a while in the summer of 1945 it looked as if perhaps the pub had closed.

We all know that democracy can be a fickle employer. But that does little to ease the pain. It's hard to be philosophical on the day after an election slips through your fingers. Clementine, trying to think of anything to say that might console her husband, looked at the returns and concluded that it might well be a blessing in disguise.

The old lion turned to his wife and said, "At the moment it seems quite effectively disguised."

"I have no regrets," Churchill told visitors in the aftermath of his defeat. "I leave my name to history." But Winston Churchill rarely did the easy thing.

He could not rest so long as tyranny threatened any part of the globe. So when Harry Truman invited him to speak at Westminster College in the Spring of 1946, Churchill leapt at the chance. He hoped that by traveling to the heartland of America he might reach the heart of America. He would do so in an address whose timeless eloquence would be matched by its indisputable logic. Churchill addressed a nation at the pinnacle of world power—but a nation unaccustomed to wielding such authority and historically reluctant to intrude in the affairs of Europe.

In the exhausted aftermath of World War II, few were prepared to listen to warnings of fresh danger.

But Churchill was undaunted. Once before, his had been a voice crying out in the wilderness against the suicidal dogmas of appeasement. Once before, he had sounded an alarm against those deluded souls who thought they could go on feeding the crocodile with bits and pieces of other countries and somehow avoid his jaws themselves. His warnings had been ignored by a world more in love with temporary ease than long-term security. Yet time had proven him tragically correct.

His Fulton speech was a fire bell in the night, a Paul Revere warning that tyranny was once more on the march.

"From Stettin in the Baltic to Trieste in the Adriatic, an iron curtain has descended across the continent," he said.

Churchill titled his speech "The Sinews of Peace," but the reaction it provoked was anything but peaceful. Newspaper editors on both sides of the Atlantic rushed to brand its author a warmonger. Labor MPs asked Prime Minister Attlee to formally repudiate his predecessor's remarks. From Moscow came a blast of rhetoric labeling Stalin's former wartime ally "false and hypocritical" and claiming that, having lost an election in his homeland, he had decided to try his luck in the United States. Harry Truman knew better.

The people of Missouri were highly pleased by Churchill's visit, and had enjoyed what their distinguished visitor had to say.

And for those trapped behind the Iron Curtain, spied on and lied to by their corrupt governments, denied their freedoms, their bread, even their faith in a power greater than that of the state—for them Churchill was no warmonger and the Western alliance no enemy. For the victims of Communist oppression, the Iron Curtain was made all too real in a concrete wall, surrounded by barbed wire and attack dogs and guards with orders to shoot on sight anyone trying to escape the so-called workers' paradise of East Germany.

Today we come full circle from those anxious times. Ours is a more peaceful planet because of men like Churchill and Truman and countless others who shared their dream of a world where no one wields a sword and no one drags a chain. This is their monument. Here, on a grassy slope between the Church of St. Mary the Virgin and Champ Auditorium, a man and a woman break through the wall and symbolically demolish whatever remaining barriers stand in the way of international peace and the brotherhood of nations.

Out of one man's speech was born a new Western resolve.

Not warlike, not bellicose, not expansionist—but firm and principled in resisting those who would devour territory and put the soul itself into bondage. The road to a free Europe that began there in Fulton led to the Truman Doctrine and the Marshall Plan, to NATO and the Berlin Airlift, through nine American presidencies and more than four decades of military preparedness.

By the time I came to the White House, a new challenge had arisen. Moscow had decided to deploy intermediate-range nuclear missiles like the SS-20 that would threaten every city in Western Europe.

It never launched those missiles, but fired plenty of trial balloons into the air, and it rained propaganda on the United States and the Federal Republic of Germany in an effort to prevent the modernization of NATO's forces on West German soil.

But the government in Bonn was not deterred. Neither was the rest of Western Europe deceived. At the same time, we in the United States announced our own intention to develop SDI, the

Strategic Defense Initiative, to hasten the day when the nuclear nightmare was ended forever and our children's dreams were no longer marred by the specter of instant annihilation.

Of course, not everyone agreed with such a course.

For years it had been suggested by some opinion makers that all would be well in the world if only the United States lowered its profile. Some of them would not only have us lower our profile—they would also lower our flag. I disagreed. I thought that the 1980s were a time to stop apologizing for America's legitimate national interests and start asserting them.

I was by no means alone. Principled leaders like Helmut Kohl and Margaret Thatcher reinforced our message that the West would not be blackmailed and that the only rational course was to return to the bargaining table in Geneva and work out real and lasting arms reductions fair to both sides.

A new Soviet leader appeared on the scene, untainted by the past, unwilling to be shackled by crumbling orthodoxies. With the rise of Mikhail Gorbachev came the end of numbing oppression. Glasnost introduced openness to the world's most closed society. Perestroika held out the promise of a better life, achieved through democratic institutions and a market economy. And real arms control came to pass, as an entire class of weapons was eliminated for the first time in the atomic age.

Within months the Soviet empire began to melt like a snow-bank in May.

One country after another overthrew the privileged cliques that had bled their economies and curbed their freedoms. Last month Germany itself was reunited, in the shadow of the Brandenburg Gate and under the democratic umbrella of NATO. I know something about that neighborhood. Back in June 1987 I stood in the free city of West Berlin and asked Mr. Gorbachev to tear down the wall.

Was he listening? Whether he was or not, neither he nor the rulers of Eastern Europe could ignore the much louder chants of demonstrators in the streets of Leipzig and Dresden and dozens of other German cities.

In the churches and the schools, in the factories and on the farms, a once-silent people found their voice and with it a battering ram to knock down walls, real and imagined.

Because of them, the political map of Europe has been rewritten. The future has been redefined, even as the veil has been lifted on a cruel and bloody past. Just last week thousands of Soviet citizens, may of them clutching photographs of relatives who died in Stalin's labor camps, marched to the Moscow headquarters of the KGB to unveil a monument to the victims of Stalinist repression. An aging woman named Alia Krichevskaya held up a photograph of a young man in an old-fashioned high collar. She wept softly.

"This was my father," she said. "I never knew him. He was sent to Sologetsky (labor camp) in 1932, a few months before I was born, and they shot him in 1937."

In dedicating this memorial, may we pause and reflect on the heroism and the sacrifice of Alla's father and so many, many others like him. Fifty years after Winston Churchill rallied his people in the Battle of Britain, the world is a very different place. Soviet Russia is coming out of the dark to join the family of nations. Central and Eastern Europe struggle to create both freedom and prosperity through market economies. How pleased Sir Winston would be!

Let me conclude with a special word to the students of Westminster College, the empire builders of twenty-first century. Before you leave this place, do not forget why you came. You came to Westminster to explore the diversity of ideas and experience what we call civilization. Here you discover that so long as books are kept open, then minds can never be closed. Here you develop a sense of self, along with the realization that self alone is never enough for a truly satisfying life. For while we make a living by what we get, we make a life by what we give.

Tragically, many walls still remain to endanger our families and our communities.

Later today the Fulton Optimist Club will join with others in recognizing winners of an essay contest called "Why Should I Say No to Drugs?" Obviously Fulton cares about its future as well as its past. Above all, it cares about the children who represent that future.

In Fulton, Missouri, as in London, Berlin, or Los Angeles, the future is what you make it.

Certainly it was unreasonable for a sixty-five-year-old parliamentarian, his counsel rejected until the emergency was at hand, to believe that he could defy the world's most lethal fighting force and crush Hitler in his Berlin lair.

It was unreasonable to suggest that an ancient church, all but destroyed by enemy bombs, could be reconstructed five thousand miles away as a permanent tribute to the man of the century. It was unreasonable to hope that oppressed men and women behind the Iron Curtain could one day break through to the sunlight of freedom—and that the Soviet Politburo itself would yield to people in the streets.

All this was unreasonable. But it all came true. My fondest wish is that each of you will be similarly unreasonable in pursuing Churchill's objectives—justice, opportunity, and an end to walls wherever they divide the human race.

Shortly before he died, Sir Winston received a letter from his daughter Mary. "In addition to all the feelings a daughter has for a loving, generous father," she wrote, "I owe you what every Englishman, woman, and child does—liberty itself." We owe him nothing less.

In dedicating this magnificent sculpture, may we dedicate ourselves to hastening the day when all God's children live in a world without walls. That would be the greatest empire of all.

And now, let me speak directly to the young people and the students here. I wonder yet if you've appreciated how unusual—terribly unusual—this country of ours is.

I received a letter just before I left office from a man. I don't know why he chose to write it, but I'm glad he did. He wrote that you can go to live in France, but you can't become a Frenchman. You can go to live in Germany or Italy, but you can't become a German, an Italian. He went through Turkey, Greece, Japan, and other countries. But he said anyone, from any corner of the world, can come to live in the United States and become an American.

Some may call it mysticism if they will, but I cannot help but feel that there was some Divine plan that placed this continent here between the two great oceans to be found by people from any corner of the earth—people who had an extra ounce of desire for freedom and some extra courage to rise up and lead their families, their relatives, their friends, their nations, and come here to eventually make this country.

The truth of the matter is if we take this crowd and if we could go through and ask the heritage, the background of every family represented here, we would probably come up with the names of every country on earth, every corner of the world, and every race. Here is the one spot on earth where we have the brotherhood of man. And maybe as we continue with this proudly, this brotherhood of man made up from people representative of every corner of the earth, maybe one day boundaries all over the earth will disappear as people cross boundaries and find out that, yes, there is a brotherhood of man in every corner.

Thank you all and God bless you all.

25

EMPIRE OF
IDEALS

At this convention, George Bush was not in the secure position that Reagan had been before his second term. Bush's popularity was dropping and he was losing the support of the conservatives within his party. That is why he brought Patrick J. Buchanan, a rival, to the podium. And he also sought to remind people of his predecessor, Ronald Reagan. Perhaps the differences in the demeanor and image of the two men explains Bush's difficulties in the White House. Even at age 81, Reagan seemed strong and was cleared a "star" of this event.

Reagan didn't disappoint the audience, delivering a trademark speech lauding the state of the nation. "Well, I've said it before and I'll say it again–America's best days are yet to come," said the former president. And the one-time actor said of President Bush, "By his own admission, he is a quiet man, not a showman."

Republican National Convention, Houston, Texas

AUGUST 17, 1992

Thank you, Paul, for that kind introduction. And Mr. Chairman, delegates, friends, fellow Americans, thank you so very much for that welcome. You've given Nancy and me so many wonderful memories, so much of your warmth and affection, we cannot thank you enough for the honor of your friendship.

Over the years, I've addressed this convention as a private citizen, as a governor, as a presidential candidate, as a president, and now, once again tonight, as private citizen Ronald Reagan.

Tonight is a very special night for me. Of course, at my age, every night's a very special night. After all, I was born in 1911. Indeed, according to the experts, I have exceeded my life expectancy by quite a few years. Now, this a source of great annoyance to some, especially those in the Democratic Party.

But here's the remarkable thing about being born in 1911. In my life's journey over these past eight decades, I have seen the human race through a period of unparalleled tumult and triumph. I have seen the birth of Communism and the death of Communism. I have witnessed the bloody futility of two World Wars, Korea, Vietnam, and the Persian Gulf. I have seen Germany united, divided, and united again. I have seen television grow from a parlor novelty to become the most powerful vehicle of communication in history. As a boy I saw streets filled with Model Ts; as a man I have met men who walked on the moon.

I have not only seen but lived the marvels of what historians have called the "American Century." Yet tonight is not a time to look backward. For, while I take inspiration from the past, like most Americans I live for the future. So this evening, for just a few minutes, I hope you will let me talk about a country that is forever young.

There was a time when empires were defined by land mass, subjugated peoples, and military might. But the United States is unique, because we are an empire of ideals. For two hundred years we have been set apart by our faith in the ideals of democracy, of free men and free markets, and of the extraordinary possibilities that lie within seemingly ordinary men and women. We believe that no power of government is as formidable a force for good as the creativity and entrepreneurial drive of the American people.

Those are the ideals that invented revolutionary technologies and a culture envied by people everywhere. This powerful sense of energy has made America synonymous for opportunity the world over. And after generations of struggle, America is the moral force that defeated Communism and all those who would put the human soul itself into bondage.

Within a few short years, we Americans have experienced the most sweeping changes of this century: the fall of the Soviet Union and the rise of the global economy. No transition is without its problems, but as uncomfortable as it may feel at the moment, the changes of the 1990s will leave America more dynamic and less in danger than at any time in my life.

A fellow named James Allen once wrote in his diary, "Many thinking people believe America has seen its best days." He wrote that July 26, 1775. There are still those who believe America is weakening; that our glory was the brief flash of time called the twentieth century; that ours was a burst of greatness too bright and brilliant to sustain; that America's purpose is past.

My friends, I utterly reject those views. That's not the America we know. We were meant to be masters of destiny, not victims of fate. Who among us would trade America's future for that of any other country in the world? And who could possibly have so little faith in our America that they would trade our tomorrows for our yesterdays?

I'll give you a hint. They put on quite a production in New York a few weeks ago. You might even call it slick. A stone's throw from Broadway it was, and how appropriate. Over and over they told us they are not the party they were. They kept telling us with straight faces that they're for family values, they're for a strong America, they're for less intrusive government.

And they call me an actor.

To hear them talk, you'd never know that the nightmare of nuclear annihilation has been lifted from our sleep. You'd never know that our standard of living remains the highest in the world. You'd never know that our air is cleaner than it was twenty years ago. You'd never know that we remain the one nation the rest of the world looks to for leadership.

It wasn't always this way. We mustn't forget—even if they would like to—the very different America that existed just twelve years ago: an America with 21 percent interest rates and back-to-back years of double-digit inflation; an America where mortgage payments doubled, paychecks plunged, and motorists sat in gas lines; an America whose leaders told us it was our own fault, that ours was a future of scarcity and sacrifice, and that what we really needed was another good dose of government control and higher taxes.

It wasn't so long ago that the world was a far more dangerous place as well. It was a world where aggressive Soviet Communism was on the rise and American strength was in decline. It was a world where our children came of age under the threat of nuclear holocaust. It was a world where our leaders told us that standing up to aggressors was dangerous—that American might and determination were somehow obstacles to peace.

But we stood tall and proclaimed that Communism was destined for the ash heap of history. We never heard so much ridicule from our liberal friends. The only thing that got them more upset was two simple words: "evil empire."

But we knew then what the liberal Democrat leaders just couldn't figure out: the sky would not fall if America restored her strength and resolve. The sky would not fall if an American president spoke the truth. The only thing that would fall was the Berlin Wall.

I heard those speakers at that other convention saying "we won the Cold War"—and I couldn't help wondering, just who exactly do they mean by "we"? And to top it off, they even tried to portray themselves as sharing the same fundamental values of our party! What they truly don't understand is the principle so eloquently stated by Abraham Lincoln: "You cannot strengthen the weak by weakening the strong. You cannot help the wage-earner by pulling down the wage-payer. You cannot help the poor by destroying the rich. You cannot help men permanently by doing for them what they could and should do for themselves."

If we ever hear the Democrats quoting that passage by Lincoln and acting like they mean it, then, my friends, we will know that the opposition has really changed.

Until then, we see all that rhetorical smoke, billowing out from the Democrats. Well, ladies and gentlemen, I'd follow the example of their nominee: Don't inhale.

This fellow they've nominated claims he's the new Thomas Jefferson. Well, let me tell you something. I knew Thomas Jefferson. He was a friend of mine. And governor, you're no Thomas Jefferson.

Now, let's not dismiss our current troubles, but where they see only problems, I see possibilities—as vast and diverse as the American family itself. Even as we meet, the rest of the world is astounded by the pundits and finger pointers who are so down on us as a nation.

Well, I've said it before and I'll say it again—America's best days are yet to come. Our proudest moments are yet to be. Our most glorious achievements are just ahead. America remains what Emerson called her 150 years ago: "the country of tomorrow." What a wonderful description and how true. And yet tomorrow might never have happened had we lacked the courage in the 1980s to chart a course of strength and honor.

All the more reason no one should underestimate the importance of this campaign and what the outcome will mean. The stakes are high. The presidency is serious business. We cannot afford to take a chance. We need a man of serious purpose, unmatched experience, knowledge, and ability. A man who understands government, who understands our country, and who understands the world. A man who has been at the table with Gorbachev and Yeltsin. A man whose performance as commander in chief of the bravest and most effective fighting force in history left the world in awe and the people of Kuwait free of foreign tyranny. A man who has devoted more than half of his life to serving his country. A man of decency, integrity, and honor.

And tonight I come to tell you that I warmly, genuinely, wholeheartedly support the reelection of George Bush as president of the United States.

We know President Bush. By his own admission, he is a quiet man, not a showman. He is a trustworthy and levelheaded leader who is respected around the world. His is a steady hand on the tiller through the choppy waters of the nineties, which is exactly what we need.

We need George Bush!

Yes, we need Bush.

We also need another fighter, a man who happens to be with us this evening, someone who has repeatedly stood up for his deepest convictions. We need our vice president, Dan Quayle.

Now, it's true: a lot of liberal Democrats are saying it's time for a change, and they're right. The only trouble is they're pointing to the wrong end of Pennsylvania Avenue. What we should change is a Democratic Congress that wastes precious time on partisan matters of absolutely no relevance to the needs of the average American. So, to all the entrenched interests along the Potomac—the gavel-wielding chairmen, the bloated staffs, the taxers and takers, and congressional rule makers, we have a simple slogan for November 1992: Clean house!

For you see, my fellow Republicans, we are the change! For fifty of the last sixty years the Democrats have controlled the Senate. And they've had the House of Representatives for fifty-six of the last sixty years.

It's time to clean house. Clean out the privileges and perks. Clean out the arrogance and the big egos. Clean out the scandals, the corner-cutting, and the foot-dragging.

What kind of job do you think they've done during all those years they've been running the Congress?

You know, I used to say to some of those Democrats who chair every committee in the House: "You need to balance the government's checkbook the same way you balance your own." Then I learned how they ran the House bank, and I realized that was exactly what they had been doing!

Now, just imagine what they would do if they controlled the executive branch, too!

This is the twenty-first presidential election in my lifetime, the sixteenth in which I will cast a ballot. Each of those elections had its shifting moods of the moment, its headlines of one day that were forgotten the next. There have been a few more twists and turns this year than in others, a little more shouting about who was up or down, in or out, as we went about selecting our candidates. But now we have arrived, as we always do, at the moment of truth—the serious business of selecting a president.

Now is the time for choosing.

As it did twelve years ago, and as we have seen many times in history, our country now stands at a crossroads. There is widespread doubt about our public institutions and profound concern, not merely about the economy but about the overall direction of this great country.

And as they did then, the American people are clamoring for change and sweeping reform. The question we had to ask twelve years ago is the question we ask today: What kind of change can we Republicans offer the American people?

Some might believe that the things we have talked about tonight are irrelevant to the choice. These new isolationists claim that the American people don't care about how or why we prevailed in the great defining struggle of our age—the victory of liberty over our adversaries. They insist that our triumph is yesterday's news, part of a past that holds no lessons for the future.

Well, nothing could be more tragic, after having come all this way on the journey of renewal we began twelve years ago, than if America herself forgot the lessons of individual liberty that she has taught to a grateful world.

Emerson was right. We are the country of tomorrow. Our revolution did not end at Yorktown. More than two centuries later, America remains on a voyage of discovery, a land that has never become, but is always in the act of becoming.

But just as we have led the crusade for democracy beyond our shores, we have a great task to do together in our own home. Now I would appeal to you to invigorate democracy in your own neighborhoods.

Whether we come from poverty or wealth, whether we are Afro-American or Irish-American, Christian or Jewish, from big cities or small towns, we are all equal in the eyes of God. But as Americans that is not enough. We must be equal in the eyes of each other. We can no longer judge each other on the basis of what we are, but must instead start finding out who we are. In America, our origins matter less than our destinations, and that is what democracy is all about.

A decade after we summoned America to a new beginning, we are beginning still. Every day brings fresh challenges and opportunities to match. With each sunrise we are reminded that millions of our citizens have yet to share in the abundance of American prosperity. Many languish in neighborhoods riddled with drugs and bereft of hope. Still others hesitate to venture out

on the streets for fear of criminal violence. Let us pledge ourselves to a new beginning for them.

Let us apply our ingenuity and remarkable spirit to revolution-
ize education in America so that every one among us will have
the mental tools to build a better life. And while we do so, let's
remember that the most profound education begins in the home.

And let us harness the competitive energy that built America,
into rebuilding our inner cities so that real jobs can be created for
those who live there and real hope can rise out of despair.

Let us strengthen our healthcare system so that Americans of
all ages can be secure in their futures without the fear of financial ruin.

And, my friends, once and for all, let us get control of the federal
deficit through a Balanced Budget Amendment and line item veto.

And let us all renew our commitment. Renew our pledge to
day by day, person by person, make our country and the world a
better place to live. Then when the nations of the world turn to us
and say, "America, you are the model of freedom and prosperity,"
we can turn to them and say, "You ain't seen nothing yet!"

For me, tonight is the latest chapter in a story that began a
quarter of a century ago, when the people of California entrusted
me with the stewardship of their dreams.

My fellow citizens—those of you here in this hall and those
of you at home—I want you to know that I have always had the
highest respect for you, for your common sense and intelligence
and for your decency. I have always believed in you and in what
you could accomplish for yourselves and for others.

And whatever else history may say about me when I'm gone,
I hope it will record that I appealed to your best hopes, not your
worst fears; to your confidence rather than your doubts. My
dream is that you will travel the road ahead with liberty's lamp
guiding your steps and opportunity's arm steadying your way.

My fondest hope for each one of you—and especially for the
young people here—is that you will love your country, not for her

power or wealth, but for her selflessness and her idealism. May each of you have the heart to conceive, the understanding to direct, and the hand to execute works that will make the world a little better for your having been here.

May all of you as Americans never forget your heroic origins, never fail to seek Divine guidance, and never lose your natural, God-given optimism.

And finally, my fellow Americans, may every dawn be a great new beginning for America and every evening bring us closer to that shining city upon a hill.

Before I go, I would like to ask the person who has made my life's journey so meaningful, someone I have been so proud of through the years, to join me—Nancy.

My fellow Americans, on behalf of both of us, goodbye, and God bless each and every one of you, and God bless this country we love.

26

10th ANNIVERSARY OF THE STRATEGIC DEFENSE INTIATIVE

In this relatively brief speech marking the tenth anniversary of the Strategic Defense Initiative, Reagan talks about how important the program and the efforts to free the world from the threat of a ballistic missile attack continue to be. He praises the many scientists involved in the creation of SDI and worked hard despite obstacles and criticism from many government officials.

Reagan stressed, "But over the years, these critics have been disproved time and time again. Today, we know that we can defend ourselves, that the threats have not disappeared–many new threats have not disappeared - and many new threats, in fact, are rapidly emerging–and that Russia and our European allies have expressed their desire to cooperate with us in developing a global system of missile defenses."

In closing, Reagan talks about the need to continue to develop whatever strategic defenses are necessary to protect the country.

Washington, D.C.

MARCH 23, 1993

G ood morning. It's a pleasure to be able to speak to you today on this tenth anniversary of my announcement of the Strategic Defense Initiative. Above all, I want to thank all of you for the hard work and perseverance you have shown through the years in supporting and shaping this very important program. It is as true today as it was ten years ago that this effort holds the promise of changing the course of human history, by freeing the world from the ominous threat of ballistic missile attack. Given the choice, shouldn't we seek to save lives rather than avenge them? I think we should. And indeed, now we can.

Ten years ago, when I asked the scientific community to give us the means of defending against the threat of ballistic missiles, I said there would be risks, and that results would take time. Well, I'm proud to say that these scientists and engineers boldly embraced this challenge, and in only a few short years broke new technological ground in developing innovative systems capable of providing effective and affordable defenses against missile attacks anywhere in the world. It is a tremendous achievement, worthy of the great scientific accomplishments of this century.

As you know, however, critics of SDI from the very beginning have been all too eager to denounce the program (and if it weren't for George Lucas, maybe we would have been off to a better start). But over the years, these critics have been disproved time and time again. Today we know that we can defend ourselves, that the threats have not disappeared—many new threats, in fact, are rapidly emerging—and that Russia and our European allies have expressed their desire to cooperate with us in developing a global system of missile defenses.

This should be good news. Unfortunately, there is a stubborn contingent of policymakers who insist on abiding by the obsolete ABM treaty and support only extremely limited missile defenses, or even none at all. Yet I believe their efforts will not stop the progress we have made and the progress we have yet to make. The wisdom of the program we launched a decade ago will prevail, and America will not remain forever defenseless against ballistic missile attack.

Now more than ever it is vital that the United States not back down from its efforts to develop and deploy strategic defenses. It is technologically feasible, strategically necessary, and morally imperative. For if our nation and our precious freedoms are worth defending with the threat of annihilation, we are surely worth defending by defensive means that ensure our survival. Thank you again. God bless you, and may God bless America.

27

LOOKING BACK, LOOKING AHEAD

Not a presidential speech per se, Reagan's comments were in response to birthday greetings made by luminaries, including his close friend Margaret Thatcher with whom he stayed in touch after leaving office. Already showing signs of what would be later diagnosed as Alzheimer's, Reagan briefly thanked the attendees for celebrating the "forty-fourth anniversary of my thirty-ninth birthday." He talked about how pleasant it has been for him to return to Washington and see many familiar faces.

Then, Reagan went on to discuss some of the achievements of his administration including cutting taxes, creating jobs, and expanding the economy. Reagan said he and Nancy remain incredibly grateful for their time in the White House. "You are those people–those great individuals who gave so much of yourselves, who sacrificed and supported us and helped us achieve everything we did," said Reagan.

Gala on the Occasion of His Eighty-third Birthday

FEBRUARY 3, 1994

I can't tell you how thrilled Nancy and I are to be here with you tonight to celebrate the "forty-fourth anniversary of my thirty-ninth birthday." Haley told me he was going to gather a few friends for dinner tonight, but I had no idea!

Before I get started here, I want to thank my dear friend, Margaret Thatcher, for being part of yet another important milestone in my life and for those very kind words. As most of you know, Margaret and I go back quite a ways. We met at a time before she became prime minister and I became president. From the moment we met, we discovered that we shared quite similar views of government and freedom. Margaret ended our first meeting by telling me, "We must stand together," and that's exactly what we've done in the years since—as friends and as political allies. Margaret Thatcher is one of the giants of our century. Her many achievements will be appreciated more and more as time goes on and history is written. For me, she has been a staunch ally, my political soul mate, a great visionary, and a dear, dear friend. Thank you, Margaret, for being with us here tonight.

I would also like to convey my personal appreciation to Haley Barbour. Haley, you and the entire Republican National Committee are doing an excellent job keeping the heat on the Democrats at both ends of Pennsylvania Avenue. Haley, back when I hired you to work on my White House staff, I suspected you might amount to something someday!

I must say that returning to Washington today really brought back memories. As our plane headed toward the airport, I looked down on the White House, and it was just like the good old days: the South Lawn, the Rose Garden, David Gergen. I looked over a couple of blocks, and there was the Internal Revenue Service—bigger than I ever remembered it. When I looked down at the enormous United States Post Office building I could just see the excitement on the faces of the bureaucrats—knowing they would soon be managing our national healthcare system! Up on Capital Hill, I saw that big, white dome, bulging with new tax revenues. I instinctively reached for my veto pen and thought to myself, "Go ahead, make my day." You may have seen President Clinton draw his own veto pen on television just last week. The difference is that his pen doesn't have any ink in it! Unless, of course, you're talking about red ink. And we all know the Democrats have plenty of that!

All of you have made our day, just by being here. It's a pleasure to see so many familiar faces and those who work so hard for the Grand Old Party. Birthdays often serve as the rare moments when we can pause from the bustle of our daily lives to reflect on the years that have passed, the accomplishments and people that have made them special. As I look around this gathering, I am filled with countless warm and fond memories. Many of you go back with us as far as my two terms as California governor. Others of you are more recent additions to the family. Regardless of when you came, you have been a big part of our lives. For that, we are so grateful and feel so blessed.

Now, as most of you know, I'm not one for looking back. I figure there will be plenty of time for that when I get old. But rather what I take from the past is inspiration for the future. And what we accomplished during our years in the White House must never be lost amid the rhetoric of political revisionists.

When we came to Washington on that bright sunny day in January of 1981, we shared a dream for America. Back then, the reach of government had become intolerable. It was a time of rampant inflation and crushing interest rates—when hope was scarce. It was a time when cold, ugly walls divided nations and human rights were trampled in the name of evil and corrupt ideologies. It was a time when the nuclear arms race was spiraling out of control and a blinding mistrust stood between East and West. We believed that for the future of America and the free world, this could not stand. And together, we insisted that this great nation must once again behave as such.

In our America, most people still believed in the power of a better tomorrow. So together we got the government off the backs of the American people. We created millions of new jobs for Americans at all income levels. We cut taxes and freed the people from the shackles of too much government. And the economy burst loose in the longest peacetime expansion ever. We brought America back—bigger and better than ever.

It was a time when America was a bright beacon of hope and freedom to oppressed people everywhere. The world looked to us—not just because of our military might—but because of our ideas of liberty and freedom. And they knew we were willing to defend and promote those ideas in every corner of the earth.

We rebuilt a demoralized, underfunded, and unappreciated military. And we made it the most modern and respected force in the world. And who can forget those so-called experts who said our military buildup threatened a dangerous escalation of tensions? What kind of fool, they asked, would call the Soviet Union an "evil empire"? But as events have shown, there was nothing foolish in my prediction that Communism was destined for the ash heap of history. After decades of struggle, and with the help of the bold leadership of Margaret Thatcher, democracy won the Cold War and the Berlin Wall came tumbling down.

The world watched with amazement as we put our house in order and took our rightful place as the most dynamic country in the world. And I firmly believe that history will record our era as one of peace and global prosperity.

However, our task is far from over. Our friends in the other party will never forgive us for our success and are doing everything in their power to rewrite history. Listening to the liberals, you'd think that the 1980s were the worst period since the Great Depression—filled with greed and despair. Well, you and I know better than that. Although the political landscape has changed, the bold ideas of the 1980s are alive and well. Republican candidates swept every major election across the country last year. From New York to Texas, from New Jersey to my home state of California. And as a result, it seems that our opponents have finally realized how unpopular liberalism really is. So now, they're trying to dress their liberal agenda in a conservative overcoat.

After watching the State of the Union address the other night, I'm reminded of the old adage that imitation is the sincerest form of flattery. Only in this case, it's not flattery but grand larceny— the intellectual theft of ideas that you and I recognize as our own. Speech delivery counts for little on the world stage unless you have convictions and, yes, the vision to see beyond the front-row seats. The Democrats may remember their lines, but how quickly they forget the lessons of the past. I have witnessed five major wars in my lifetime, and I know how swiftly storm clouds can gather on a peaceful horizon. The next time a Saddam Hussein takes over a Kuwait, or North Korea brandishes a nuclear weapon, will we be ready to respond?

In the end, it all comes down to leadership. That is what this country is looking for now. It was leadership here at home that gave us strong American influence abroad and the collapse of imperial Communism. Great nations have responsibilities to lead and we should always be cautious of those who would lower our profile, because they might just wind up lowering our flag.

My friends, on a serious note, I would like to end by telling you something Nancy and I have wanted to say to you for a long time. During our years together here, as you know, things were always on the move. As soon as we accomplished one objective, we were quickly on to the next. There was rarely time to celebrate victory or recall all the people who made it possible.

Well, one of the benefits of retirement is you get a chance to reflect back over the years. Since Nancy and I have returned to California, we've spent many occasions looking back at what we did here and remembering the extraordinary people who worked so hard to make those great days possible. And we've wondered if we would ever get the chance to thank them. You are those people—those great individuals who gave so much of yourselves, who sacrificed and supported us and helped us achieve everything we did. So I will conclude tonight by saying that the greatest gift I could receive on my birthday is to be able to stand before each and every one of you and convey in the only words I can how grateful Nancy and I are. Thank you for being there—and for being here. And thank you for making this evening a memory I will cherish forever. Until we meet again, God bless you, my friends.

28
LAST LETTER
TO AMERICA

Surprising some, Ronald Reagan bid farewell to the country with the release of a handwritten note. Accompanying the note which was circulated by his office in Los Angeles was a letter from his physician explaining Reagan had been diagnosed with early stage Alzheimer's disease. Testing for the disease had occurred over the previous year as a result of the former president's apparent memory loss and related symptoms.

Reagan, who was the oldest person to be elected president, was in good health while in the White House, recovering quickly from a gunshot wound suffered in a failed assassination attempt.

Speaking at a rally shortly after this announcement, President Clinton spoke of the former president and asked people to send Reagan good wishes.

"I now begin the journey that will lead me into the sunset of my life. I know that for America there will always be a bright dawn ahead," said Reagan.

In His Own Hand

NOVEMBER 5, 1994

———

M y fellow Americans, I have recently been told that I am one of the millions of Americans who will be afflicted with Alzheimer's disease.

Upon learning this news, Nancy and I had to decide whether as private citizens we would keep this a private matter or whether we would make this news known in a public way. In the past, Nancy suffered from breast cancer and I had my cancer surgeries. We found through our open disclosures we were able to raise public awareness. We were happy that as a result, many more people underwent testing. They were treated in early stages and able to return to normal, healthy lives.

So now we feel it is important to share it with you. In opening our hearts, we hope this might promote greater awareness of this condition. Perhaps it will encourage a clearer understanding of the individuals and families who are affected by it.

At the moment I feel just fine. I intend to live the remainder of the years God gives me on this earth doing the things I have always done. I will continue to share life's journey with my beloved Nancy and my family. I plan to enjoy the great outdoors and stay in touch with my friends and supporters.

Unfortunately, as Alzheimer's disease progresses, the family often bears a heavy burden. I only wish there was some way I could spare Nancy this painful experience. When the time comes, I am confident that with your help she will face it with faith and courage.

In closing, let me thank you, the American people, for giving me the great honor of allowing me to serve as your president.

When the Lord calls me home, whenever that day may be, I will leave with the greatest love for this country of ours and eternal optimism for its future.

I now begin the journey that will lead me into the sunset of my life. I know that for America there will always be a bright dawn ahead.

Thank you, my friends. May God always bless you.

Sincerely,
Ronald Reagan

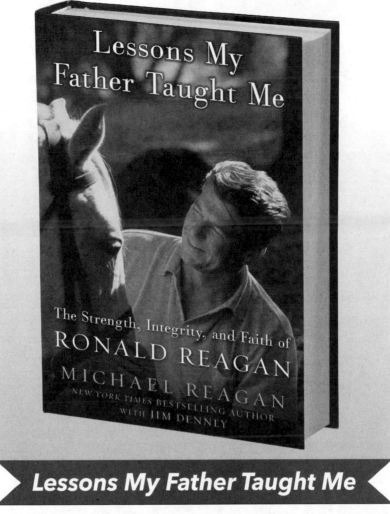